THE COMPLETE BOOK OF
PUPPETS & PUPPETEERING

Robert Ten Eyck Hanford
Illustrations by Ted Enik

Sterling Publishing Co., Inc.   New York
Oak Tree Press Co., Ltd London & Sydney

CONTENTS

**Published in 1981 by
Sterling Publishing Co., Inc.
Two Park Avenue
New York, New York 10016**

**Distributed in Australia by Oak Tree Press Co., Ltd.,
P.O. Box J34, Brickfield Hill, Sydney 2000, N.S.W.
Distributed in the United Kingdom by Ward Lock Ltd.,
116 Baker Street, London W.1**

Library of Congress Cataloging in Publication Data

**Hanford, Robert.
The complete book of puppets and puppeteering.**

**1. Puppets and puppet-plays. I. Title.
PN1972.H32   791.5'3   74-22590
ISBN 0-8069-7032-4
ISBN 0-8069-7033-2 Library
ISBN 0-8069-8970-X pbk.
Formerly ISBN 0-87749-758-3
Formerly ISBN 0-87749-845-8 pbk.**

Printed in The United States of America

Chapter 1

Puppetry: Today, Yesterday, and Tomorrow

Puppetry Today

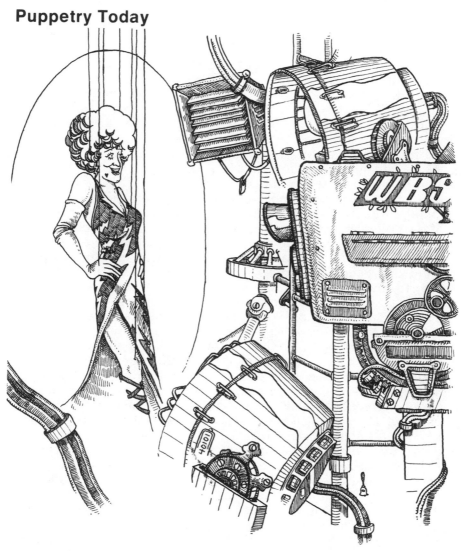

The current status of the art of puppetry in the United States leaves much to be desired. The theatrical establishment, educational institutions, and the general public still need to be enlightened about the art of puppetry.

3

In Europe, where television is less influential, live entertainment (ballet, opera, theatre, concert and puppet productions) is still widely popular. In America, however, performing arts have suffered generally from the increased reliance of the public on television for its entertainment. The only real market for most puppeteers has been live children's theatre; hence, puppetry has become identified as a child's entertainment.

To make matters worse, many amateur showmen who claim to be puppeteers have abused puppetry by presenting poorly written and under-rehearsed programs for children. Naturally, parents who take their children to such shows aren't going to be impressed with puppetry as an art form. Bad puppet shows are then attributed to a weakness of the art itself, rather than to the individual performer or group.

Only a small percentage of the adult population has seen the best live puppetry has to offer, because few organizations can afford what full-time artists must charge to cover their expenses and make a living. Luckily, with the aid of grants, subsidies, and affiliations with large institutions, some talented puppeteers have been able to perfect their art. But most free-lance puppeteers cannot support themselves from bookings. They often must work at part-time jobs elsewhere, or starve.

Many potential sponsors consider a fee of several hundred dollars outrageous for an hour long presentation. They don't realize that what appears to be an hours' fun is actually a full day of labor (including getting all the equipment to the site, setting up, striking the stage after the performance, and transporting the equipment back home). They also don't appreciate that the show has to be written and rehearsed, the set built, and the puppets themselves designed, built, costumed, and kept in good repair. Most puppet companies in this country must seek grants and affiliations with institutions. The number of staff members must be kept to a minimum. In the European countries that generously subsidize puppetry, large staffs of specialists can be employed. The self-employed puppeteers of the United States must be jacks of all trades. Not only do they have to be talented actors, but they must have diverse technical know-how as well. Unlike a performer in the so-called legitimate theatre, who walks in to do the show and then leaves, puppeteers must be their own stagehands as well—loading, unpacking and setting up a stage, then performing, and then dismantling the stage and taking it home. Being a puppeteer requires incredible physical fitness as well as talent.

Yet, despite all these hardships in a humble profession, puppeteers are dedicated artists determined to see that puppetry achieves the status it deserves. Puppetry is not an obscure branch of theatre; *it is theatre*, as legitimate as Broadway and perhaps more so. The slick commercial brand of theatre found in the United States today is very young compared to the long-standing heritage of puppetry.

Why is puppetry a second-class art? Perhaps because it looks so easy. Anyone can put on a puppet and be silly. But to really master the art of puppetry requires the mastery of many separate art forms. Talents from many areas must be pooled creatively. It takes a lot of valuable time to find a combination that works. In our "Crank-'em-out-as-quickly-as-possible" society, fields that don't yield the maximum dollar per unit hour remain unexplored. This has left puppetry (with only a handful of exceptions) in the realm of a children's craft. Puppetry is not only a child's medium, but a medium for all those with active imaginations. Puppets are so fantastic for kids because in their fantasy-oriented minds they can produce an extravaganza with extremely simple puppets and sets.

Economy of form and dialogue are also extremely important in professional puppetry. The minds in the audience should have to work to fill in the details. However, this doesn't mean that puppeteers can shortchange their audiences. The concept of the show must be consistent, thoroughly explored, and thoroughly developed. Which details the audience is to fill in must be carefully planned, not accidental. Technically, the production should be as perfect as possible; but most important, the production should be good theatre. In other words, it should appeal to the emotions of the audience and sustain their interest. To be a valid art form rather that a trite exercise, the production should be a personal statement about life. A professional puppeteer must dig deep within his or her own self to find a feeling that comes from the heart. In short, the production must have soul.

Although I sense that the situation is changing in this country, too many puppeteers have entered the field from the craft side and are very ignorant of the dramatic considerations. All too often puppetry is taught as an art course; once the puppet is built, the lesson stops. In reality, this is where the puppeteering begins. The puppet is a tool that can only be appreciated in the context of the entire production. A puppet does not reach its full glory until it comes to life in the imagination of the audience.

Puppets are actors; hence, puppeteers must have acting ability. For a long time, stage actors have looked down upon puppeteers. But more and more actors are discovering something important they can learn from puppets. This is the importance of letting the audience do its share of the work. If everything on stage is completely defined the audience becomes a group of uninvolved observers. Puppets are able to hold the attention of the audience because they only represent life in an abstract way. They are not real—but the audience makes believe they are. Likewise, live actors need to know how to make an audience create reality out of what is represented on stage.

Puppetry has been picking up many new fans in recent years, and many of them (at long last) are coming from the theatre world. This trend is undoubtedly due to the innovations and excellence of one group of puppeteers who have done more to popularize puppetry in the United States than anyone in the past: The Muppets.

The Muppets

The names Jim Henson, The Muppets, and Sesame Street are so well-known among fans of puppetry that I really wonder how much introduction they need. Big Bird, Bert, Ernie, Grover, Oscar the Grouch, Kermit the Frog, Cookie Monster, and all the other puppets seen daily on Sesame Street have truly won the hearts of this country. Their success is envied by all puppeteers, and the Muppet style of puppet has inspired countless others.

What is it about the Muppets that makes them so special? Is there a formula—a magic recipe—that could turn the average puppet group into as successful a company as the Muppets? The answer, I believe is Yes—but the ingredients are very rare and hard to come by. Consider the following: Take one part administrative genius and add sheer talent and unique creativity. Then blend tastefully with equal amounts of endearing personality and dynamic charisma. Next allow these ingredients to interact by adding liberal doses of money. Finally, age several years with national television exposure and continual hard work. If you can do that you'll be hot on the heels of the biggest thing to hit puppetry and television in general. You'll also find yourself in the inescapable position of being compared to your predecessor. Hopefully, you'll have found your own style and you won't be labeled a cheap imitation of the real thing. However, the Muppets have set a standard and the public wants nothing less. The standard is perfection.

Obviously, before you ever get into a television studio you must have an excellent product. The problem, in terms of the professional world of television, is how to capture that product on tape. All the acting talent, fantastic designs, brilliant scripts, and merry melodies will be in vain if it can't be recorded with perfection. Many talented specialists are required behind the scenes to make it happen. Jim Henson and director Jon Stone are able to make it work.

I visited the Sesame Street set on a Friday, the day the Muppet inserts are taped. (Monday through Thursday the street scenes are taped, but Friday is reserved for the puppets.) At 9 A.M. everybody had arrived and the set was up for a five minute Super Grover bit. Shortly thereafter, puppeteer and camera run-throughs were conducted. The camera people learn where the action will be and the puppeteers learn where the cameras will be framing their shots. By 10 A.M. a taped run-through was tried, but there were still some problems. The tape was played back and everyone watched as Jon Stone gave instructions to his talent and crew. They tried it again, and again, and again—until they got it right. Once they had a satisfactory version, they taped it a few more times just to see if they couldn't get it *better*. By Noon it was getting stale, so a lunch break was declared. In the afternoon a new skit would be tried on a different set—a whole day for two short pieces of tape. Such liberal studio time is an expensive luxury; indeed, the big television dollars are, without question, a key element in the Muppet success story. However, money alone can't produce quality; it takes creative genius to put it all together, a top notch staff of specialists (as found at Jim Henson Associates and Muppets Incorporated), and the remarkably diverse talents of Jim Henson.

Jim Henson developed the Muppet type of puppet before he went to college at the University of Maryland. He never did puppets as a child, but between high school and college he started doing a local television show in Washington, D.C., called "Sam and Friends." This was basically a five minute, adult oriented comedy show, aired twice each day. At first he didn't do any voices—only pantomimes to records; gradually, over the eight years the show was on the air, he started writing his own material and doing his own voices. In his freshman year at college he took a course in puppetry, where he met his wife Jane who was one of the founders of the Muppets in the beginning.

Two things contributed to the uniqueness of the Muppet style, according to Henson: first he knew no other puppeteers (although he admits being influenced by, and a big fan of Bil Baird, Shari Lewis, and Kukla, Fran, and Ollie); second, the original Muppet characters were designed for television closeups. Most puppeteers start by performing live before an audience, but the Muppets began on television. According to Henson, this gave "a different sort of focus—a different starting point—and therefore our style developed along different lines."

Henson experimented with the usual puppet-building materials (plastic wood, carved wood, and fabric) before discovering the flexibility and skin-like quality of foam rubber. He has tried casting foam rubber, but "it's generally more trouble than it's worth." Instead, his Muppet designers still work primarily by his original method of using contact cement to glue pieces of polyfoam together.

"Sam and Friends" led Henson to the production of a series of commercials for the Wilkins Coffee Company. Later, the Muppets were seen on variety shows—Ed Sullivan and Rowlf became nationally popular on the Jimmy Dean show. Shortly thereafter (1969) the Muppets began doing the puppets for a new television program, "Sesame Street."

"Sesame Street" is the product of The Children's Television Workshop. (C.T.W. is a separate organization from the Muppets, although the Muppets are often referred to as "The Sesame Street Puppets.") In the words of C.T.W. founder and president Joan Ganz Cooney, "The Children's Television Workshop was created to find out whether the immense appeal and impact of television could be effectively directed to the education of young people." C.T.W. started in May, 1968, but did not broadcast its first program until November, 1969. In the interim, extensive research was conducted to develop the program format. It was determined that the audience would be preschool children, with the emphasis on youngsters from disadvantaged homes. Since their research showed that commercials hold the attention of children, C.T.W. decided to use short skits to teach the alphabet and numbers. Animation and puppets were among the visually stimulating devices to be used.

The Neilson Surveys indicate that 9 million children watch Sesame Street each year. With a saturation level of 97 per cent of homes in the poor neighborhoods in Chicago, Sesame Street has become a "Ghetto Institution."

On January 15, 1975, I went to the New York office of Jim Henson to question him about the Muppets and his career. The following is a partial transcript of our discussion.

Have the Muppets developed and grown as you expected when you first started?

Well, it's hard to know what to expect when you first start. My first few years I did puppets because it was something nice and fun to do while I was in school. I had been in it for a couple of years before I ever took it seriously at all. I was in it for a while, and then I went to Europe for a summer and met a number of European puppeteers. I became enthused with it as a form—a theatre form. At this point I felt there was a lot I wanted to do with puppetry. I'm just beginning to get into that stuff.

Are you satisfied with having specialized in puppets or are there other areas you'd like to branch out to now?

Oh, not yet. For most of my career I kept my filmmaking going—doing art films and other things with images. I just stopped that four or five years ago. I will undoubtedly return to it at some point; but right now it feels like the time to concentrate on puppetry.

Where do you want the Muppets to be in ten years?

I think there are whole areas of puppetry that we haven't done yet; that we've been talking about, and that I've wanted to do but haven't been able to do.

How about feature films?

We've wanted to do that. As part of our deal with A.B.C. we have development of some properties toward a feature film.

I've heard you described as the Walt Disney of the '70s. What do you think of that?

I think that's a bit exaggerated. I don't ever see myself as Walt Disney, or any entrepreneur. It won't happen. Walt Disney was a different sort of thing. I really don't think I'm interested in being great big like that.

When you do a television "special," are you in control of the script material and content, or are you given the script?

Well, it varies. When we appear on a special—Herb Alpert, Julie Andrews—we work with another producer, and the material is subject to the producer of the show. Usually, I'm the key person in what it is and that sort of thing. I'm not just subject to it. A show that we do ourselves, like this last special, which I produced—then we control all the script materials and so forth.

Do you find it easier to create shows with particular stock Muppets in mind, or do you prefer to concieve of a show and invent characters as needed?

A combination. Certain characters that have been built up over a period of time are very solid characters. I know them well and I know how to write for them. Generally, for a certain piece of material you'll want new characters, and it's more fun to create characters just for that piece of material. Some of those characters may be good enough to last, and become stock characters.

What would happen to a Sesame Street Muppet character if the puppeteer were laid up in a hospital for a long time?

Generally, we'd be able to schedule around it because the shows are taped so far in advance. When people have had health problems, we generally have been able to work around their schedules. On the first season I replaced Big Bird on one show, and none of us were terribly happy with the results.

What would happen if one of your puppeteers just couldn't continue puppeteering with you?

Well, then we would certainly change. We'd audition people until we found a voice that was close, and so forth.

So the character really exists in the puppet and the concept, rather than in the puppeteer and his interpretation?

Oh, yes. The puppeteer changes the character a great deal, and certainly if you changed the puppeteer on any of those characters the character would undergo a change. But, it's like a soap opera, too—it's bound to undergo a change. I think the kids would accept it. We have made major changes in the puppets and I think they've accepted it.

Is it true that no one besides a Muppeteer can try on a Muppet?
    We generally try to do that, yes. In the past we've had some bad experiences. We state it as a rule just to make it clear to all the people who ask, "Can I put that on?" because we don't want—you know the problem, you're a puppeteer.

Where do you draw the line between a puppet and a costume?
    I don't. I think that puppets, masks, costumes, marionettes, and hand puppets can mix around. There's no real line.
Do you think Sesame Street would have made it without the Muppets?
    Oh, I'm sure it would have. It would have made it in a different way and it would have been a different show, but it's awfully hard to tell.

Is there any one person to whom you owe most of your success?
    No, I don't think so, no *one* person. There are a number of influences—people like Shari Lewis, Bil Baird, Burr Tillstrom, Stan Freberg, and others.

Sesame Street's Cookie Monster is a Muppet character that requires two puppeteers. Frank Oz supplies the voice and manipulation of the head and one hand. A second puppeteer (usually Richard Hunt) manipulates the remaining hand.
Courtesy Muppets Inc., NYC.

Sesame Street's Grover is a hand and rod Muppet performed by Frank Oz. (Grover is seen here without his Super Grover costume.)
Courtesy Muppets Inc., NYC.

Jim Henson, creator of the Muppets, and Kermit the Frog, star of his own television special.
Courtesy Muppets Inc. NYC.

Oscar the Grouch is also one of the regular Muppet characters from Sesame Street. There are actually two Oscars. One has the regular controls for the lower jaw and eyebrows; the other also has a special mechanism to turn the eyes left or right in their sockets. The latter Oscar is used less often because of the complexity of the controls.
Courtesy Muppets Inc., NYC.

The characters on Sesame Street. This daily one-hour program, created and produced by the Children's Television Workshop, is seen by an estimated 9 million children on nearly 300 television stations throughout the United States.
Courtesy Children's Television Workshop, NYC.

The Bad Guys from the television special, The Muppet Musicians of Bremen. *The heads and hands of these characters are polyfoam covered with flocking fuzz.*

Puppetry Yesterday

In his book *The Art of the Puppet*, Bil Baird proposes that masks became associated with magic when they effectively disguised hunters seeking food. Thus, divinity became a central part of ceremonies in which successful hunts were acted out by masked dancers, in hopes of guaranteeing the success of the next hunt.

The first puppeteer may have been a priest who discovered he could hinge the jaw to his mask and fool his peers into believing it was alive. The addition of strings to objects used in rituals performed in dimly lit caves served the same function. Again, the tribe was fooled and the great priest became greater because his magic had induced the spirits to visit the totems and bring them to life.

Unfortunately, very few artifacts of ancient puppetry have survived. We know that the ancient Egyptians use puppets, as evidenced by the moving statues found in the ruins of shrines. But we can only speculate about how they were used. Figures on strings are mentioned in documents of the ancient Greeks and Romans, but we know nothing of the content of the plays that were performed. Clearly, however, puppets, in one form or another, have been with us since the beginning of civilization.

Different cultures have evolved different kinds of puppets. Many of the ancient forms have been passed down from generation to generation and are now part of the cultural heritage of India, Turkey, Indonesia, Japan, and China. In some cases the puppet shows were basically slapstick, geared to the common audience, and full of blatantly sexual scenes. There were also highly refined performances produced for the enlightened nobility.

It is a testament to the universal appeal of puppets, that they have been making people laugh for thousands of years. Puppets also have been used to educate people and to comment on the political and social mood of the day before universal education.

Shadow Puppets

The oldest puppet shows that bear a resemblance to those performed today were probably silhouettes set to motion on the tents of the early nomads. These crude shadow puppets most likely had no moving parts. Yet a storyteller, with the aid of a campfire, could easily jiggle the cutouts to entertain the tribe on the other side of the tent wall.

The addition of dangling limbs was the next logical step, but it was not until the limbs had control rods attached that a major breakthrough in puppetry was accomplished. With the development of puppet animation through control rods, the emergence of three dimensional puppets was just around the corner—give or take a couple of hundred years.

Three distinct types of shadow puppets were used in ancient Turkey, China, and India. Though of similar construction—leather cutouts that cast shadows on translucent screens, operated by control rods—the movement, size, style, manner of operation, and content of the plays give each type unique qualities.

Eastern Shadow Puppets. The *Tholumatta* shadow puppets of southern India are extremely large (four to five feet), and made of nonviolent leather (from an animal that has died a natural death, not been slaughtered). They are delicately pierced and colored and are supported by a vertical rod. The legs hang loose but the hands have rods attached to them. The tales presented deal with numerous gods and demons and go on all night in the temple grounds.

The *Wayang Kulit* figures of Java (Indonesia) are more delicately pierced than Tholumatta. Men watch the shows on the side of the screen with the operator, and they see colors and designs drawn on the puppets. Women watch only from the front and see only the shadows. These puppets are about two feet high; the plays are much the same as those performed in India. Again, the main support rod comes up from the bottom and travels through the figure of the puppet.

Far Eastern Shadow Puppets. There are two main kinds of Chinese shadow puppets: The northern, or Pekingese, and the southern, or Cantonese. Both are notable for the very delicate lines and beautiful colors achieved by staining the hide; the Cantonese puppets are bigger, and made of thicker leather. The main support for these puppets does not come vertically from the bottom. Instead, a rod is attached at the neck. This allows the puppets to have legs that swing clear to simulate walking. The hands also have rods attached, allowing them to be moved. The heads are removable and interchangeable. The heads are always removed after the performance because of a superstition that the puppets might otherwise come to life at night.

All Chinese puppet plays are involved with the history and folklore of the people. Classic tales about heros and battles, women and lovers, and emperors and enemies are very popular. Religious overtones are not as prevalent in the plays of the Chinese Shadow Theatre as in the Indian (predominately Hindu).

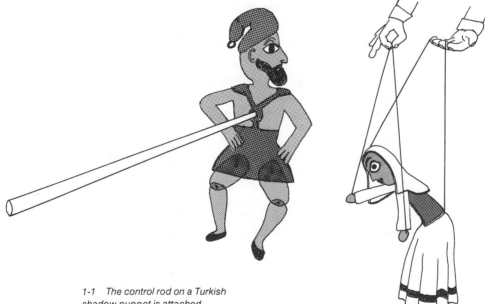

1-1 The control rod on a Turkish shadow puppet is attached perpendicularly. Note also that the joints on the legs allow them to swing freely.

1-2 A Kathputli marionette couldn't be simpler. Only two strings are used by the puppeteer.

Turkish Shadow Puppets. The transluscent colored figures made popular during the Ottoman Empire are operated by rods that attach perpendicularly to a hole in the upper half of the body (I-1). This

enables the puppets to bend over and do somersaults with ease.
Unlike shadow puppets with vertical support rods, they can't do an
about face, but the rod can be attached to either side so that the
puppet can face left or right.

The shadow puppet Karaghoiz (a clown hero) is so beloved that the
entire style of theatre is recognized by his name. The Karaghoiz
puppets have legs that dangle freely. Joints at the hips and knees give
them this movement. Occasionally a hand has a control rod, but
usually the hands are rigidly attached to the body in a fixed position.

In a royal court, Karaghoiz was well-mannered and knowledgeable
about the finer things in life. However, in the burlesque cafes of
Turkey, Greece, and Northern Africa, Karaghoiz was a crude and
boisterous scoundrel. Much of the humor centered around
Karaghoiz's oversized phallus and his popularity with women.

String Puppets And Rod Puppets

As the early civilizations of the East and Far East left their boarders
to explore new lands, they undoubtedly borrowed the new puppet
techniques they encountered. The exact chronology of the
development of three-dimensional puppets is unknown, but the
puppets and marionettes of today have obvious roots in certain older
forms.

Wayang Golek Rod Puppets. This Indonesia, shadow puppet (still in
existence today) was three-dimensional rather than flat. Support came
from a vertical rod extending down from the puppet. The operation of
the arms was also much like its flat counterpart, the Wayang Kulit.

The pre-Hindu characters are mostly clowns, grotesgue in design.
The later Hindu plays were not comic in nature. The characters usually
represented good, evil, and other human virtues (not unlike the
Medieval Morality Plays).

Rajasthan String Puppets. In the north of India we can still find the
centuries-old Kathputli marionettes that have only two strings. One
string supports the puppet; the other controls the hands (1-2). The
puppets have no legs, but instead wear floor-length pleated kilts.

These puppets have a unique language—actually high squeaky
sounds created by the puppeteer with a bamboo and leather reed held
in the mouth. (This device is known in England as a "swazzle," and is
the distinctive sound associated with Punch and Judy shows.)
Although the Kathputli speak no actual words, the people of
Rajasthan India (and foreign visitors too) can understand what the
puppets mean to say.

Sicilian Puppets. An interesting combination of marionette and rod puppet is found preserved in Sicily. The puppets are controlled from above, like marionettes, but thick iron rods are used instead of string, because of the size and weight of these heavily armored puppets. The operator supports the body of the puppet by holding a hook on the end of the rod that extends down to the head or neck. Another rod, attached to the hand, is used to make the puppet fight with a sword.

These puppets are often called Orlando marionettes in honor of the hero of the epic tale *Orlando Furioso*. Orlando is a knight whose courage knows no limit. The central attraction of an Orlando marionette performance is the numerous fight scenes in which the puppets noisily attack each other. At the end of a battle scene slaughtered puppets lay strewn about the stage, piled several high, many decapitated.

Chinese String Puppets. There is no form of traditional puppetry that can't be found somewhere in the long history of China. The marionette is no exception. The Chinese marionette stood aproximately two feet high and had a great number of strings. These strings were attached to a paddle that had a hook on the upper side to hang up the puppets not in use. The numerous strings were used to animate the eyes, mouth, eyebrows, and fingers of the puppets.

The puppets were used to enact historic tales and folklore, as were the Chinese shadow puppets. A cloth backdrop and a low proscenium hid the puppeteers. They stood at stage level and leaned over the backdrop to operate the puppets. Scenery was seldom used.

European Marionettes. In Europe during the Middle Ages, wooden figures controlled with strings became a popular part of church services. Miracle Shows, as they were called, commonly depicted the Assumption of the Virgin and the Story of the Nativity. The name *marionette*, meaning "little Mary," is derived from these church puppets.

As the popular performances became more and more comic, they moved into the church courtyard and eventually into the public squares. The guilds took over from the monks, and eventually the performances became so rowdy and vulgar that puppets were no longer used in connection with church services.

Hand Operated Puppets

Banraku Puppet Theatre of Japan. A unique style of puppetry, dating back over three centuries, the Banraku puppets were recently declared a National Treasure of Japan. Their classical performances have the status and respect that opera has in the west. Japan had other forms of puppets before the Banraku, and modern forms have been developed since. However, the beauty and grace of Banraku performances continues to reign supreme today.

Each principal character in a Banraku play is operated by three puppeteers. The main operator controls the head with his left hand and the right hand of the puppet with his right hand. One assistant controls the left hand and another assistant controls the feet. The puppets are held directly in front of the puppeteers, who are visible; by convention, the audience ignores their presence. The assistants wear black hoods over their heads, but the main operator's face can be seen.

It takes a long time for a Japanese puppeteer to reach the status of a main operator. An apprentice usually begins on secondary characters that only require one operator. Then he advances to the feet of a principle character, and eventually graduates to become a "left-hand man." Finally, after more than twenty years of apprenticeship, he is ready to become a main operator.

Since a narrator tells the story and supplies all the dialogue, Banraku puppeteers are only manipulators. It takes a great deal of practice and coordination for the trio of puppeteers to work closely as a team. The body movements are extremely graceful, almost balletic, and the faces are very expressive. The main operator holds the head on a stick that has many levers to animate the eyebrows, eyes, and sometimes even the jaw of the puppet.

Great care is taken in the crafting of these puppets and the main operators are very proud to prepare the costumes for each performance. Banraku puppeteers are not trained to perform puppets of both sexes; they must choose to operate either male or female characters and stick to that sex for their entire career.

Chinese Hand Puppets. The hand puppets of ancient China were manipulated by one puppeteer who did all the work, including voices and occasional sound effects. The puppeteers used a small booth or bag-like stage, large enough for just one person. Certain stages could stand free, attached only to the puppeteer (whose feet were visible below the fabric of the bag booth). Other stages were supported by a single pole, leaned against a building or a wall for stability.

The puppets were small, and snugly fit the hands of the puppeteer. Bamboo and silk reeds were occasionally used to provide the characters with squeaky voices, like Karaghoiz and Punch.

Punch and Judy. Punch did not join forces with his wife and the baby until after 1688A.D. However, the ancestry of Punchinello, the hook-nosed humpback clown, goes back to the Italian Commedia Dell'Arte of the 1500s.

Originally brought to England by an Italian string puller, Punch is classically a vain and brutal scoundrel. Although commonly thought to be mainly an English creation, the same character can be found, under different names, in Russia, Czechoslovakia, Hungary, and

Germany. His name may be different, but his personality is essentially the same wherever he is found. His voice alone, distinct from the other characters who appear with him, is created with a reed (*swazzle*) in the puppeteer's mouth. The fundamental reason for his popularity, in spite of his bad habits, is that as a puppet he is able to do and say all the things that we can't. He satisfies our fantasies by beating up the landlord, the police, his wife, his child, the judge, the hangman, his dog, and even the devil himself.

Punch did not take on his violent nature until he became a hand puppet in the eighteenth century. Before that, as a marionette, he was not as effective at picking things up (like clubs) and throwing them around. His wife Judy (who was known as Joan until the early 1800s) usually took the brunt of his temper fits, although she got her licks in too. Many of the Punch and Judy puppets that have been saved (and not buried with their puppeteers) still bear the battle scars and chipped paint of these family squabbles.

Puppetry Tomorrow

Obviously, I can't predict what's going to become of puppetry in the future. But speculation on the future, based on the present, is possible. Therefore, this chapter concentrates on present trends which can be safely extrapolated to provided clues to the future status of the art of puppetry.

The Puppeteers of America, Inc.

The Puppeteers of America has been (and I'm sure will continue to be) a major influence in North American puppetry. It is a society open to everyone working with or interested in any form of puppetry. P. of A. has held national festivals each year (except during World War II) since its founding in 1939. In recent years, these festivals, held each year in a different area of the country, have attracted approximately 500 amateurs, professionals, and hobbyists. Current P. of A. membership runs over 2,000 persons.

Life at a week-long puppetry festival is truly bizarre. People from all walks of life have only one thing on their minds: Puppets. Husband and wife puppet teams, church puppet groups, professional companies, famous, semi-famous, and beginning puppeteers all try to attend the festival each year. Workshops and performances are held during the day. Two major evening productions are given by renowned professionals from the U.S. and abroad.

The underlying goal of the P. of A. is to raise the quality of puppetry in America. The official publication, *The Puppetry Journal*, is received by members bi-monthly. Articles of specific and general interest keep members in touch with each other and the scope of their craft.

Local puppetry guilds are also an important part of the Puppeteers of America. Presently, there are about twenty four active puppetry guilds which have meetings, workshops, and performances. (See Appendix for a list of guilds.)

The future status of American puppetry is largely up to the individuals who comprise these organizations. Without nationally affiliated guilds puppeteers would have little chance to exchange ideas and learn what their fellow puppeteers are doing. Attenting guild meetings or puppet festivals is a good way to increase one's motivation to do better work. By seeing the work of others, beginners are inspired to work harder. Established puppeteers also become more dedicated to improving their skills when they see up-and-coming talent that will soon be competition.

UNIMA

The international equivalent of the P. of A. is UNIMA, *Union Internationale De La Marionette*. Puppeteers from throughout the world unite in this organization. The UNIMA conferences are held primarily in Europe. Puppet companies from different countries compete for awards at these conferences.

Jim Henson is the chairman of the American Center of UNIMA.* According to Henson, the main thrust of the organization is to unite the professionals and practitioners of the art, and the American Center also exists primarily to serve the needs of the professionals. Nevertheless, membership in UNIMA is open to amateur and professional alike, and Henson doesn't feel that anyone is trying to drive the amateurs out of UNIMA.

In recent years there has been some concern over the quality of the shows representing the United States at the UNIMA conferences. Almost anyone who could afford to take a show to Europe was able to perform at them. In Europe, and especially Eastern Europe, where puppetry is highly respected, the productions presented at a conference are the best a country has to offer. The United States was sometimes "laughed at in eight languages" because no screening procedures had been established and no official entry designated.

In an effort to improve this situation, a committee of UNIMA members has been established to give citations to outstanding American productions. It is assumed that these citations will be viewed as a seal of approval particularly for troupes performing abroad. Thus sub-standard productions will no longer be able to represent the United States. This kind of unified effort will certainly improve the status of American puppetry.

Foreign Puppetry

Study of puppetry undoubtedly will lead puppeteers to seek information about foreign traditions. My curiosity about contemporary foreign puppet companies led me to the discussion with Bil Baird printed here. Admittedly, we only scratched the surface of a subject about which volumes could be written. All the same, I found what he had to say very interesting. I hope this segment will whet your appetite, and that eventually you will want to travel to see the puppet theatres of various countries.

What is puppet theatre like in the Communist countries?

Well, in the Communist countries they depend a great deal on production, partly because they are strictly censored as to what they can say in the theatre. I believe China has the strictest limitations. I've seen Chinese puppet plays, and they certainly show that they have limitations. They just do propaganda, propaganda, all the time. However, that means that they must try to put on spectaculer productions with lots of color.

They have gigantic companies, don't they?

Right. There are very few companies over there with fewer than thirty-five people. They even carry their own live orchestras sometimes. Certainly, their stagehands and puppeteers are specialists, and they do carry an awful lot of equipment.

The Russians, who have had very little string tradition, carry a fairly complicated hand puppet stage, just a little taller than the people who operate it. Most of these Russian operators are not very tall—they don't have tall skinny people like we do.

Other countries, like Czechoslovakia, Rumania, and Germany, that started out with string marionettes, had to make compromises when they transferred over to rod puppets. Their stages will accomodate both because they've made pits in their stage floors.

One of the most interesting stages I've seen was in Prague. It was a hand and rod combination, built like a set of steps leading down into a pit towards the audience. To picture it, suppose you start with a level stage floor where you would have a theatrical performance with live actors (not that puppets aren't live). Then imagine that walking towards the audience down a set of steps into a hole in the stage. The operators stand on different levels, dressed in black. Each one or two has a special spotlight operator following his puppet from the side.

You mentioned the Russians . . . .

Yes. Obraztsov in his Moscow Theatre has two permanent companies. He has something like 300 people on his staff, most of them specialists. Of the two companies, one is on tour all the time; the other plays in the theatre. The size of the stage in his permanent theatre is identical to the one that tours. In fact, they built him a new theatre recently—he's been that successful and influential. They consider him a very important person. He plays to kids part of the time, but mostly he plays to adults. He has a double-barrel theatre there. One has about 800 seats; the other, about 400. Any production will fit in either theatre, or it can tour. That is like my set-up here in New York City.

I suppose portability of the stage is not a big concern of the large foreign companies.

Well, the simplest stage I ever saw was made by the Bulgarians, who were doing a rod puppet show. They simply stretched a rope across a regular big legitimate stage, pulled a curtain across on that, and then performed behind the curtain. I presume they propped it up in a few places during the show, but you couldn't see that.

They set this up in front of the audience?

In front of us, yes. Everybody came out in black leotards. First of all, they set up a sort of jungle gym and put into it the elements of what they were going to do. This was World War I stuff, so they brought out an old Victrola and they played *Valencia* on it. They had a Matisse painting and things they set up to establish the era, but then they took them away.

What was the scenery and lighting like?

The scenery was just sort of little flats, and the lights were all from the side.

They didn't use the existing theatre lights from the front?

No, they brought their own lights. There was a little from the front, but mostly they were using theatre lights from the side.

This wasn't black theatre technique, was it?

No, no, these were just lit from the side. Their puppets were made of cardboard tubes, with hats, and fur, and things like that. They had the faces painted right on them like cartoons, and they held them up in the air. That's one of the things they have to do—inasmuch as it is very hard for them to say anything, they have to go into production in a big, big, way.

Puppetry in Education

Using puppets to teach is not new. The ancient shadow shows taught popular folk tales to the illiterate masses. Even the rowdy Mr. Punch made his audience think about the social and political ills of the day.

I do believe the educational uses of puppetry will receive considerably more and more attention in the future. Shows like Sesame Street have proven the effectiveness of puppets, hundreds of puppeteers will undoubtedly be jumping on the bandwagon. There is, however, some controversy about how this will affect puppetry as pure theatre or pure art form.

I have spoken to several puppeteers who are not happy with the idea that promising new talent will become absorbed in the educational uses of puppets. They would prefer the top creative minds to make breakthroughs in the area of live adult entertainment. The argument is not without foundation.

Grant money flows much easier to persons wearing educational hats. Contrarily, those carrying a torch for pure theatre can't boast the utilitarian benefits of education. As a result, we have the classic case of the artist selling out to the patron. Long ago, when the churches and the nobility supported artists what they produced had by necessity, to please those sponsors. Today, if the money is going to come from those in favor of educational puppet shows, you can bet your swazzles that there will be more puppets teaching than you can shake a control rod at.

Nevertheless, don't forget that much fine art was produced under the sponsorship system. Just because the subject matter is controlled doesn't mean the artist need be hindered. My guess is that puppets put to work teaching will pave the way for the acceptance of puppetry as valid theatre. Foundations will sponsor education, but as a fringe benefit the public will (hopefully) be given good theatre too.

It is worthwhile to stop and consider why puppets are so useful in the learning process. Children may learn from building puppets, using puppets, or watching puppets. The common denominator here is that puppets are fun and hold a child's attention. Long instructional presentations can be interrupted with puppet skits to make them less tiresome. Audience participation is easy with puppets, and no child has to be coaxed to become actively involved.

Puppets are very effective propaganda agents for adult audiences also. In Latin American countries, United States AID missions use puppetry as a visual aid in the agricultural extension program. The agents there could never openly criticize the stubborn old farmers, but puppets are able to say what people can't. Mobile puppet theatres have been particularily effective, because the shows presented about health, nutrition, or farm practices can adapt to the unique cultural patterns of each rural community. Local politicians can be worked into the scripts, and specific problems emphasized. Films cannot be tailor-made to the individual needs of a village.

In a conversation with Peter Schuman of the Bread and Puppet Theatre, I mentioned that in a particular project of that time I was using puppets to teach basic music theory to elementary school children. He claimed, to my surprise, not to like puppets teaching because it was "too sneaky"—despite the fact that the Bread and Puppet performances had mainly anti-war and anti-establishment themes. (I suppose it's not propaganda unless you disagree with the message. Certainly his shows were trying to sway public opinion in very subtle ways. If that isn't "teaching" in a "sneaky fashion," then I don't know what is.)

In an effort to present a broader view than my own about the future of puppetry, I asked many professional puppeteers if they had any comments.

Nikki Tilroe, of the Frog Print Theatre (Ontario, Canada):

The variety of uses that puppets can serve would seem to offer quite an opportunity for puppeteers this year, next year, and in the years ahead. New forms and media, including electronic forms such as television, laser, computer technology, fiber optics, etc, all offer potential for future puppet experimentation. With a solid background in puppetry technique, with understanding of how we as human beings express ourselves interpersonally and how we communicate effectively with an audience, and with knowledge of how we can shape and transform matter in space to entertain and enrich the sharing of imagination, the future of puppetry can be an exciting dimension of our culture, on an equal par with other art forms.

Bruce Chesse of the Mount Diablo Unified School District (Walnut Creek, California):

I see the future of puppetry in education because it has the ability to integrate human relations, positively criticize and clarify concepts through illustration, and to create a climate more conducive to learning. Puppetry creates an environment more in harmony with the world in which the child lives from day to day. Once exposed, there is no reason why this interest cannot be carried over into adulthood. After all, puppetry has a universal appeal for all. We need only to direct people's attention.

Jim Henson Muppets Inc. (New York City): Do you think the legitimate theatre people will recognize puppetry as valid theatre soon?

I think it's up to us to do valid theatre and then they'll recognize it. The responsibility is with the puppeteers. Any good puppetry will encourage good puppetry and any bad puppetry will discourage all puppetry.

Do you think the advent of video cassettes in the home will help puppetry?

Not particularily. It's a medium in which to work. Maybe it will create more television programming material, in which case you can say there will be more input, but it's hard to tell. I don't think it's going to make a major change in anything, because there is a lot of access right now in terms of local television program origination and syndicated program origination.

How will you feel if the new generation of puppeteers work primarily with the Muppet-type of puppets? There's a lot of that already.

Yes, we find that interesting. I have mixed feelings about it. I sometimes resent certain things that come on looking very much like our work. But I'm getting over that, because a lot of our work is now becoming generic. With Sesame Street having been on the air five years now, a lot of kids are growing up knowing no other puppets but ours. When those kids get older, I think they will create much more of our kind of puppetry—and it's nice, it's really okay. In general, I think all puppeteers would do better to discover styles of their own, just as I think that the reason we were able to make our mark was that we came up with something different. I think that's true of anybody. The person who comes up with something in a different form and style will be recognized more easily.

What excites you the most about the future of puppetry in America?

The work that I'm doing, of course. If it weren't that way, we'd all be in bad shape.

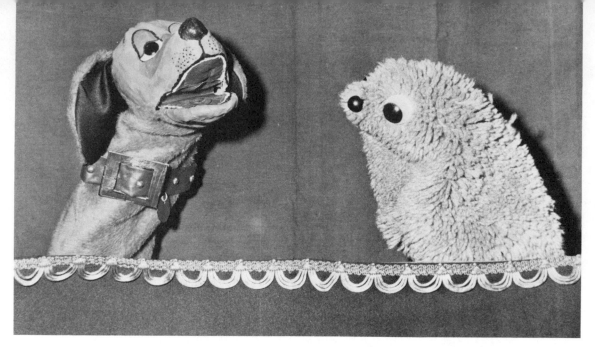

Buster the Dog and Corky the Caterpillar, two hand puppets with mouths built by One Way Puppets of Pompano Beach, Florida. These characters are from a play designed to teach children the value of prayer.

Courtesy Bob Dolan, Pompano Beach, Fla.

Fabric puppets by Puppet Productions, San Diego, Calif.
Courtesy Bill Hawes, San Diego

It's much easier to watch the puppets if the backdrop is thin enough to see through.
Courtesy Betsy Glassman, Ithaca, NY.

Sonia Manzano (better known as Maria) with Bert, a hand & rod Muppet from Sesame Street. Bert is made of foam pieces covered with colorful fuzzy fabric. Flawlessly neat construction is required on Bert and all Muppets designed to be seen close-up on television.

Courtesy Children's Television Workshop, NYC.

Neatness counts when the puppets will be seen close up by a TV or film camera. These puppets were designed for stop motion animated filming by Dan Peeler for Bill Stokes Associates, Dallas, Texas. Photo by Don Stokes, courtesy of Dan Peeler

Silhouettes on a translucent screen are an ancient puppet medium. This scene, by Joe Ayers, is far more sophisticated in design than the early shadow figures, but the basic principle is the same. Photo by Larry Cooper, courtesy of Joe Ayers, Johnson City, NY.

This shadow scene, from Joe Ayer's production of Sir Gawain and the Green Knight uses both positive shadows (above) and negative shadows (below).
Photo by Larry Cooper, courtesy Joe Ayers, Johnson City, NY.

This Polyfoam lion from the Poko
Puppets presentation of Aesop's Fables
shows an imaginative use of foam balls
and fabric pom poms.
Photo by David Attie, courtesy of
Larry Engler-Poko Puppets, Roslyn
Heights, NY.

Texas Punch, made by Dan Peeler
of Dallas Texas. This latex rubber puppet
was made for the Lone Star Puppet
Guild.
Photo by Don Stokes, courtesy Dan
Peeler

Rod puppets from the New York
Jazz Museum's Jazz Puppet Show,
featuring the Poko Puppets. Note that
only the trumpet needs a rod because
the hands are sewn in place.
Courtesy Larry Engler, Rosyln Heights, NY.

A Polyfoam puppet built by the
Puppet Theatre Workshop class at
Ithaca College. Spray paint is applied
directly to the surface of the foam.
Courtesy Robert W. Bonnell, Ithaca, NY.

Larry Berthleson with rod puppets from the Pickwick Puppet production of Sleeping Beauty. *These tall puppets are designed for large theatre performances.*
Courtesy Ken Moses, Pickwick
Puppets, Fairview NJ.

Beauty and the Beast, plastic wood rod puppets by Dick Myers. Although his puppets don't have animated mouths or eyes (let alone pupils), the audience is perfectly able to imagine these details. The heads can turn left and right or nod up and down, and with these movements he is able to suggest speaking. The arms and legs can also be animated by levers (below) on the main support rod.
Courtesy Dick Myers, Hyde Park, NY.

Peter Zapletal's Beauty and the Beast, *which has been aired several times nationally on Public Broadcasting Service (PBS). Peter Zapletal is puppetry producer for the Mississippi Authority for Educational Television.*

Chapter 2

The Tools of The Trade

There are two main tools a puppeteer needs in order to perform: puppets and a stage. This chapter outlines a variety of ways to start a puppet theatre.

Basically, there are two classes of puppets: those that are made by the puppeteer and those that are bought in a store. There are also two kinds of puppet stages: those that are meant to travel and those that are permanently located. Each kind has its advantages and disadvantages. Consider your own needs before deciding which type of stage and puppets are best for you.

Buying Puppets

You may already own a puppet or two, but let's consider for this discussion that you are starting from scratch, and that you want puppets with which you can perform. This is an important consideration. Almost any toy store carries puppets, but most of them are not meant for performing. The majority of commerically available puppets are really toys for young children. They may be durable, washable, and very cute—but they are horrible puppets. Those mass-produced, felt or stiff plastic puppets may be great for little children to play with on the family room floor, but that's all they were designed for. They're just dolls you can stick your hand into and move around. They don't necessarily respond well to your hand at all.

If you intend to use a puppet seriously, try it on before you buy it. It's your hand that will bring the puppet to life, so you want a puppet that fits your hand well. If it's too small, your actions will be cramped. If it is too large, you will have trouble keeping it on and controlling it.

With a hand puppet, your fingers should reach all the way into the tip of the glove (2-1). Otherwise, when the puppet picks something up in a play he will be doing it with his wrists instead of his hands. The pocket that receives the tip of your finger should be just snug enough to keep your fingers from slipping out. If it's too snug it may take two hands to put the puppet on, which *could* be a problem during a performance.

When you are performing with puppets you are bringing an inanimate object to life. In the minds of your audience the puppet is alive. A good puppeteer always tries to keep this illusion from being broken. Naturally, the better your equipment works for you the easier your job will be. Each time your performance is interrupted by some technical difficulty audience attention leaves the imaginary world you and your puppets have created, and instead focuses on the backstage machinery, and the reminder that there is actually a person back there running things. Think of your puppet as a tool that you can use to fool the audience. This tool, or instrument, should be simple and efficient. The more complex the mechanism, the harder it is to operate. Of course, practice makes perfect; but a good general rule for the

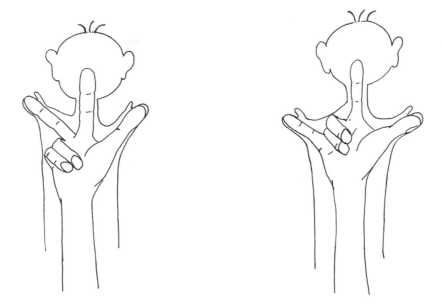

2-1.   It is best if the tips of your fingers reach all the way into the tip of the glove. The illustration on the left shows the most common way to wear a hand puppet. The method shown on the right has the advantage of providing the puppet with shoulders of equal height. However, since this second method requires strong pinkies, the first method is best for beginners.

beginner is: the simpler the better. Therefore, most of this book deals with hand puppets. Once you've learned the basics of puppeteering with hand puppets, you'll be ready for more complicated kinds of mechanisms. But hand puppets themselves can be quite challenging, and you may find yourself sticking with them. When you eventually get good enough to present large public performances you'll want hand puppets bigger than most available in stores. However, in the beginning your audiences should be small and no one will have problems seeing your puppets.

The two biggest manufacturers of quality hand puppets are Steiff and Kersa. Steiff makes mostly animal characters, and Kersa mostly people stereotypes. Unfortunately, both have short sleeves that cover only the hand. It is advisable to lengthen the sleeve so that it extends to the elbow. A short sleeve may reveal the puppeteer's wrist during a performance if the puppet has to bend over or reach high for something. Lengthening the sleeve is relatively simple on the Kersa puppet but more difficult on the Steiff puppet, which has a fake fur body that can be hard to match. If you cannot find the fake fur (or the proper color for a Kersa puppet) to match the body you may be able to make a sleeve extension that looks like pants or a skirt for the puppet, depending on what type of character the puppet is. Sometimes clothes are acceptable on an animal character; but if the animal character has human traits (such as speech), clothes may enhance them. This is the central structure of animated cartoons.

Since Steiff and Kersa puppets are relatively expensive (five dollars and up), you'll want to start out with a small and flexible collection. Starting a puppet theatre can be prohibitively expensive if you try to get too much equipment and too many puppets at the very beginning. Instead, I suggest that you first buy just one boy and one girl puppet. The next two characters to add to this collection would be an old man and an old woman. If you can afford to buy all four right away, fine—but if you're like most people (including myself) your collection will grow slowly. In my case, each new addition to my stock company was made after much scouting around. Usually the decision to buy a particular puppet was made long before the actual purchase. When you go shopping for puppets, you will see many attractive speciality types—detectives, Indians, ghosts, devils. I don't recommend purchasing these stereotypes at the beginning. They're good only for particular roles and will limit your choice of script material. Plain puppets can become new characters if you just stick a hat and coat on them. If your friendly neighborhood toy or book store carries only speciality character types, look for ones that can be converted easily to plainer types. Often, the hat or cape are held on by only a few threads. Once the specialty trimmings are removed—if they can be removed—you'll likely find a plain puppet underneath. Be sure to check whether the puppet has a full head of hair beneath the hat. Sometimes they have only a few strands of hair at the edge of the hat to suggest a full head of hair. Removing the hat will then leave you with a bald puppet. Of course you can always make hair for a puppet, but a peek under the hat before you buy can save you trouble.

Any trimmings you remove should be saved. You can always use them to make the puppet back into the original character. You also can use them as patterns to make new hats or capes or whatever. By designing and constructing new trimmings you'll be able to create new characters far more easily (and less expensively) than by buying (or building) a large cast. A boy puppet can be a peasant, a prince, a brother, a thief—or even become an adult with the addition of a moustache and beard. A girl puppet can be a princess, a sister, a shopkeeper, or Gretel, Goldilocks, Little Red Riding Hood, Sleeping

Beauty. The old man can be a father, a mad scientist, a king, a crook, a merchant, a grandfather. Likewise, the old lady can be a grandmother or a mother, a witch or a queen. With these four characters you'll be well on your way to producing any show you want.

Eventually, you will start to increase the size of your collection. Keep in mind, though, that you should not buy what you can easily make. For example, a witch is easy to make. If it comes out ugly and deformed, all the better! On the other hand, a really elegant queen can be quite hard to make, and so might be worth buying. Exactly what characters you add after the initial four puppets is entirely up to you. You may find, after performing a number of skits or shows, that one particular puppet is often needed to play two characters. If you're constantly making costume changes, you should seriously think of acquiring one of those two characters for your collection. For instance, your old lady puppet is very busy playing both the witch and the queen. You might choose to solve this problem by adding a witch puppet to your collection, since you can build one yourself. Or, if you really like the design of the witch's costume, and are less happy with the queen's you probably would choose to buy a new queen puppet. But these are decisions you will have to make for yourself, based on your own assessment of your own needs and situation.

Although I cannot tell you in what order you should acquire puppets, or whether you should buy them or make them as an intermediate step, I do suggest, filling out the characters of a royal court. Please note that there is no rush in completing this cast. Your collection should increase to meet your needs, and the full cast is only a guideline for you to consider. It is not essential equipment needed to start a puppet theatre. As a matter of fact, I don't even have all the characters for a complete cast in my own collection. The process of acquiring new items for the collection is all part of the fun. But the special charm of a puppet collection is that each character has its own unique personality. The fact that you are the one that gives them their personality creates a special attachment. Even the animal characters tend to have their special ways, whether or not they speak. So remember: if your collection grows slowly it's all for the best. You need time to establish a strong, definite, unique personality for each new character you acquire.

A cast of ten characters might consist of the original four puppets plus six new ones (two of which could be animals). This collection has grown to a very comfortable size (2-2). The addition of a prince, a princess, a king, and a queen would leave the original four puppets to become any group of supporting characters. They might be a peasant family to be contrasted against the royal family; they might actually be characters of the royal court; with the help of costume changes, they might be both. To get an idea of the dramatic potential of this cast,

2-2   *A growing puppet collection.*

imagine the situations you can create by contrasting characters: thief *vs.* shopkeeper, magician *vs.* witch, brother *vs.* sister, prince *vs.* peasant, king *vs.* magician. Conflict creates action in drama and puppetry is no exception. An almost endless number of skits can be improvised just by contrasting characters. Furthermore, the two animal characters will enable you to consider the production of many traditional folk tales that includes parts for animals. Kingdoms always seem to be plagued by some sort of beast, and peasant families often have pets which bring them good or ill fate. Animal characters are especially good when very young children are to be involved in a production. Delivering lines can often be difficult for young puppeteers, but growling and gobbling people up suits even the youngest extremely well.

Be sure to consider the ages of those who will use the puppets when you are buying them. In general, the younger the puppeteer, the rougher the treatment of the puppets, so plan accordingly. If you try to get youngsters to take special care of fragile puppets, you'll only end up frustrating them and yourself. Young kids have a marvelous spontaneity, but this "live-for-the-moment" spirit makes it hard for them to relate to the long range bad effects of leaving puppets on the floor, in the sandbox, etc. Washable or vinyl puppets will solve the problem. However, if an older sibling or adult will be working with the production, part of the collection can be kept apart and brought out only during supervised sessions. For the most part, common sense is all that's needed to take good care of puppets—but it's important to make the effort to use your common sense. For instance, puppets not in use should be stored so that the costumes won't get wrinkled and creased. This is best done by hanging them upside down, or on a series of short vertical dowels stuck in a board. Do not leave them in a box, one on top of the other. Pick a storage area free from dust, direct sunlight, moisture, or mildew. Keep them well out of reach of pets unless you want a mangled collection. These are greater precautions than one might take with most toys, but I hope you realize by now that puppets are more than toys. Any small tear or hole in a seam in your puppets should be mended immediately. Good puppets, well cared for, can last through years—even generations—of service, and may even become collectors items. I noticed that two of my oldest Kersa puppets are not featured in the most recent catalogue. If they are permanently discontinued mine will soon be rare objects, because each Kersa character is entirely handmade and produced in relatively small quantities. But since their real value to me is as members of my cast, it's not likely I'd ever sell them anyway.

A complete cast of puppets would add a jester, a witch, a lady-in-waiting, a wizard, a dragon, an ogre, a frog, and a duck to the intermediate collection. With this "dream collection" there's practically no story you can't do. If you want to keep increasing your puppet collection, you can add any specialty characters at this point. Frankly, I feel the time and money would be better spent producing accessories to turn the original four puppets into any specialty characters you might require. The advantage to a large complete cast is that your productions can have a snappy, lively pace when you don't have to stop for costume changes—although you can achieve wonders with a clever script and assistants to do the changes. But there is one thing you really can't change—the puppet's face. If the audience can recognize the same face on two supposedly different characters, they may get confused. With a large cast, each character's face can have unique features and a shape all its own. Keep this in mind if your cast is small and you're doubling up on characters. Be sure to disguise the face as completely as possible. Many puppet heads can accept pins as well as a pin cushion. Using pins, you can securely fasten such disguise as glasses, hair, false noses, moustaches, and beards.

Although the large cast makes a puppeteer's life much easier, transportation and storage problems do increase. But these problems are fairly easily dealt with. The real problem is financial. To buy a cast of twenty at $7.50 each will cost $150.00 plus tax. You can build your own for a fraction of that amount. If you are willing to invest the time. However, if you've just recently become curious about puppets, I strongly recommend that you buy the first four puppets. You have enough new things to contend with without learning how to make puppets as well. Later, once you're into the swing of things, you can discover how much more fun it is to use puppets you've created yourself.

Building Puppets

Building puppets is a creative endeavor. I cannot tell you what to do because I don't know you; nor is it likely that I would, even if I did know you. People work in ways as various as their personalities. When I was teaching puppetry at Ithaca College, Salvatore Grippi (Professor of Fine Arts) told me to regard teaching as an act of love. He was referring to the fact that to coach someone's creativity is a very delicate matter, requiring knowledge of and sensitivity to the individual's personality. Everyone has the potential to make beautiful puppets, no matter how uncreative he thinks he is. It's my belief that everyone is creative, but some people haven't learned how to use their creativity or have had it stifled at some point in their lives. If you think this applies to you, making puppets may be just the therapy you need to discover that you really are creative after all. Obviously, some people are more creative than others—but give yourself a chance, and you just may surprise yourself.

It's very hard to teach (or learn) puppet building without the materials in front of you. Therefore, the first thing I suggest you do is to seek out persons (or groups) in your area who are involved with puppets. You can learn an incredible amount about puppet construction just by trying on various puppet types. Better still, if you can see puppets being built you will get a good idea of how difficult or easy what you have in mind will be to realize.

Design Considerations

What I said before about buying puppets applies even more to handmade puppets: the simpler the better. Gimmicks such as moving eyes or eyebrows, jumping hats, and wiggly ears are nice extras, but a beginning puppet builder should concentrate on making an efficient and neat basic puppet. There's no sense in having a really nice gimmick in a puppet that otherwise doesn't work too well. If the puppet is poorly constructed, or just plain ugly, no one will be impressed that the eyebrows work. But don't worry, your craftmanship will get better as you gain experience. Eventually you will be ready to tackle more complex designs.

The age of the builder quite naturally makes a difference in the way the finished puppet will look. In general, children have a shorter attention span than adults, the younger the child, the shorter the span. The job to be tackled should match the ability of the builder to stick to it and eventually complete the task. Children should be able to see some results of their efforts almost immediately. If there are too many preparations to be made, and too many steps with long waits between, a young child is likely to get bored with the project. With this in mind, I designed a simple puppet for which elementary school children could finish the head within five minutes. With the heads completed they were inspired to complete the bodies, because they could see they were not too far from the finished thing. To hasten the construction of the bodies, masking tape was used to hold the seams together—not a very permanent method, but easy and quick. The kids were more interested in playing with the puppets than crafting them well, so this design, which took only half an hour to complete, was perfect.

Another important consideration is the coordination of the builder. Young hands often cannot perform the tasks that young imaginations might wish. By necessity, the tools and materials used must match the sophistication of the user. This will directly affect the results.

Although, I said before that everyone is creative, not everyone has the same amount of native creativity—the amount of curiosity, imagination and patience inherent in a person. Some people have a great deal, and others must work to cultivate what they have.

Obviously, your creative ability will affect your final results. Don't be afraid to make mistakes. The artist who is curious enough to experiment is the one who discovers something new and exciting. Too many people want everything they create to be portfolio-perfect, and this attitude inhibits the imagination. So what if your sketches aren't suitable for framing—you may just find something in those doodles that you like. So you take the idea and you imagine ways to rework it. You change this, or that, or vary something else. Eventually you'll either discard the idea entirely, file it away, or use it.

Patience also will affect the quality of your work, because quality is directly proportional to the amount of time spent on the work. If your patience is short you may rush your work to finish quickly—and it's likely the end result will look rushed. If you find it hard to sit down for long stretches and work on a project, you should try working on more than one project at a time. Then when you get bored with a particular one you can put it down and pick up another. You may put a project down, and come back to it later and wonder why you even started it. Don't throw it away when this happens—file it. You may return to it later, convinced that it wasn't a bad idea after all—or with the realization that it was an interesting idea, but not worth the time it would take to complete. It's much easier to be objective after some time has passed since the moment of inspiration. Then you can really commit yourself to following through to the end. That commitment is the most important ingredient of good work. If you lack patience, it will show up in your end product.

As you gain building experience you will gain confidence as well as technical ability. Both affect the quality of your work. When you're just starting out you are likely to be apprehensive about your work. A puppet master has enough experience to have built up his confidence; he knows that his errors often can be covered up. For instance, once when I was nearly finished with a puppet I accidentally ripped a hole next to the mouth. I fixed the hole easily enough, but the face was scarred by the repair work. So, I added a nice, thick, black moustache, which hid the repaired area completely.

It is important for the novice puppet builder to remember that everyone makes mistakes, and that one learns from one's mistakes. The trick is to know when you've made a mistake. Sometimes you won't know until you've finished the puppet; eventually, you should be able to forsee problems and deal with them before they happen. This kind of experience will help to increase your confidence.

The more puppets you've made, the faster you will be able to work without sacrificing quality. You will know what works and what doesn't; you will know when it is important to work slowly. It is easy, sometimes, to grow so eager to see the finished results that you rush your work. I have often spent time trying to work around a design flaw that would not have presented itself had I taken a little more care at the beginning. You will find yourself thinking more carefully as you gain experience. For example, individual parts should be painted before they are attached—but most people have to learn this the hard way.

Experience in performing with puppets is essential to the crafts person who wants to make good puppets. An artist who has never put on a puppet show may be able to sketch ideas for new puppet characters, but he will be lost when he must translate the sketches into working, three-dimensional puppets. Until you have used puppets on stage you won't have a sense of the specifications to which the design must conform—the "performability" of the puppet. However, there are some basic concepts which can help the novice puppeteer move more quickly to the discovery of the basic characteristics of a performable puppet. This is not to say that performing experience will no longer be important, but rather that you will have a head start.

As I stated in the section on buying puppets, a puppet that *only* looks good is suited for the display case. The performability of a puppet should be considered on the basis of three criteria: durability, mobility, and flexibility.

The durability of a puppet is basically the strength of the material from which it is made and how strongly the individual parts are attached. Puppets made of polyurethane foam, for example, can tear easily if you're not careful. Foam also rots over a period of time. Plastic, wood or celastic are, on the other hand, very durable.

The mobility of a puppet is the action of which it is capable. Certain types of puppet hands are useless with props; others handle them well. Some puppets have heads capable of up-and-down and back-and-forth motions; other heads are stiffly mounted (on a rod) Sometimes costumes severely limit the motion of the puppet; the basic frame itself may be stiff and immobile. Ideally, a puppet should be able to do whatever you may want it to do.

The flexibility of a puppet is the ease with which it may become more than one character. Costumes and features that are permanently attached create an inflexible puppet. The most flexible puppets I know are the *anything Muppets*. These puppets are just bodies with mouths, to which any features and clothes can be attached (2-3).

Your familarity with the different kinds and styles of puppets can also affect your work. If you have handled and studied the control mechanisms on marionettes, rod puppets, and shadow puppets, you will be better able to adapt and combine the mechanical principles they use when designing controls of your own. The more puppets you have seen the more familiar you will be with costuming methods. Seek out puppeteers in your area. Occasionally you'll run across a company or a puppeteer with a gimmick that is kept a well guarded secret, but most puppeteers love to show off their creations. Bring your sketchbook—but be sure to get permission to take notes on the

THE ANYTHING MUPPETS

Here's a group of puppets that can become almost anything! The possibilities are endless.

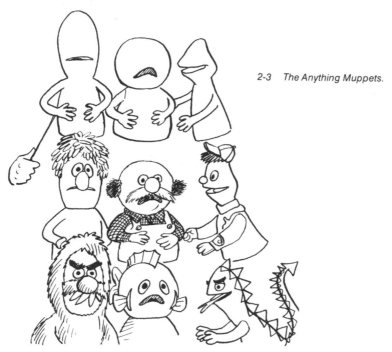

2-3   The Anything Muppets.

Illustration by Carol Spinney

puppets they show you.

Your style as an artist will also be influenced by other people's work. Therefore, it is enriching to become familiar with as many styles of puppets as possible. If your inspiration is too narrow, their influence may be all too apparent in your work, and you may be labelled a copy rather than an original.

The tools at your disposal will have a very definite effect on your results. Power tools make your work go faster, allowing you to concentrate your efforts elsewhere. Although hand tools can always get the job done, you should at least investigate the availability of the following: drill press, band saw, electric sander, sewing machine, compressed air paint sprayer, and radial arm or table saw. Remember that you can always rent such equipment. If you do rent, it's a good idea to line up all the work ahead and then rent on half-day rates.

If you don't sew, get friendly with someone who does. Otherwise you'll be limited to costumes made of felt. Felt can be cut and glued; you don't have to worry about hemming, because felt has no threads to unravel. However, felt is not suitable for all costumes; sooner or later, you will need the services of a sewing machine. Ask your friends who sew to teach you. Even if they offer to do the sewing for you, try to learn the basics so you will understand the construction and can get the results you want.

The time available to you for work on a puppet will affect your final results. As I said before, quality is directly proportionate to the amount of time spent on the piece. Sometimes even the most patient craftsman is rushed to meet a deadline. The truly dedicated, usually sacrifice sleep before sacrificing quality. However, lack of sleep and overwork are sure ways to fray nerves, causing short tempers and arguments between you and your associates. The best way I know to allow enough time to complete a task is to use my father's formula. Hanford's Law works as follows: add up all the hours the task could possibly take, allowing for mistakes, delays, extra trips to the store, etc. Multiply your answer by three and you'll have an accurate estimate of how long the task will really take.

Deadlines are a problem for both the full-time and part-time puppeteer. The advantage a full-time puppet builder has over the part-time builder is that he can accomplish the same task in a matter of days instead of weeks. However, the part-time builder can take much longer to work on a project, because it's not his sole source of income; the full-time artist is usually under more pressure to meet deadlines and economize on the amount of time devoted to any one task. Therefore, the professional must rely on his knowledge and experience to enable him to do high quality work in a short period of time.

The degree of perfection required of the finished product makes a big difference on the outcome. If you are not really motivated to do neat work it is unlikely that your puppet will conform to high standards of neatness. However, neatness may not always be required. Children use their imaginations to make up for the neatness they may lack. If a puppet is not intended to be seen close up, it will not require the neatness of, say, a television puppet. The closeup lens of a television camera can reveal the tiniest flaws in painting or sewing. Building puppets for television requires a perfectionist.

Often, more than just surface neatness is required. The basic mechanics and design of the puppet must be perfect if the highest degree of performability is to be achieved. Your goals will be determined by the use for which you intend the puppet. If, for example, the character has only a small part, perfection of performability may have a low priority. On the other hand, if the character is to have a leading roll in your cast, your motivation for all-around perfection will be reflected in your final results.

The desired life expectancy of the puppet is another factor that will affect your final results. Is the puppet built to become a permanent member of your cast, or is it needed for just a very short time? Your answer will most likely affect your choice of materials and methods of construction. I've used glue, masking tape, or even staples for a costume needed for a one-time videotape session. Such temporary construction methods cannot be relied upon for puppets needed over longer periods. If the puppet must be durable enough to last for years the materials must be chosen and used appropriately.

Wood, celastic, paper maché, and plastic wood are very strong, but they are also somewhat difficult to work with. Styrofoam balls and polyurethane foam are easy to work with, but fragile unless covered. If fabric is used to cover puppets made of polyfoam the deterioration caused by exposure to air and sunlight will be slowed down. (If you've ever run across an old pillow or cushion make of foam, you'll know what I mean by deterioration. The foam turns yellow and begins to crumble to dust.) To get the most out of foam puppets, put fabric on the inside also, (or wear cotton gloves) to absorb the sweat from your hand. Styrofoam can be covered with a variety of things to make it stronger. Uncovered, it dents rather easily. However, plaster, paper maché, or felt can be applied to the surface to protect it.

The size of the finished puppet is determined by the use for which it is intended. If the puppet is to be used on television, it can be almost any size. If it is to be used in a large public performance, however, it should be as large as possible, so that it can be seen clearly by everyone. Size is limited only by performability. The puppet should not be so large that it is unmanageable. The controls must be appropriate for the size and weight of the puppet. As the puppet becomes larger, keeping the individual pieces light in weight becomes more critical. This in turn affects your design and choice of materials, which automatically affects your final results.

Instructions

#1. *Quickie Hand Puppet.*

This design is ideal for young children with short attention spans. The entire puppet can be completed in a half hour, and the head takes only five minutes. The construction is not very permanent, but it enables the children to have puppets to play with in a hurry. Later on, a helpful mother can strengthen the puppet by removing the masking tape and sewing the seams of the body.

Materials

One styrofoam or polyurethane ball, 3″ to 6″ diameter; four colored thumbtacks with long shafts; two self-adhesive colored circles; fake fur or yarn; one 3 × 5 file card; white glue; masking tape, 1″ minimum width; fabric.

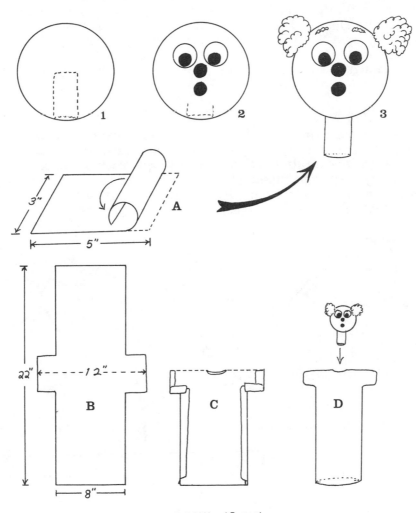

2-4 *Quicki Hand Puppet.*

Directions

With a scissors, hollow out a finger hole in the ball (see 2-4, diagram 1). Next apply the circular colored dots where the eyes will go, and then stick in the four colored thumbtacks (2-4, diagram 2). Third, take the file card and roll it around a pencil (2-4, diagram A). Allow the tube to loosen to the size of the puppeteer's index finger. Tape the tube to keep it this size. Attach the hair with glue or pins and glue the tube into the finger hole (2-4, diagram 3). While the tube is drying in the head, cut the fabric for the body as shown (2-4, diagram B). If the children are very young, have these patterns precut. Fold the fabric over (dotted line) and seal all the seams except the bottom with masking tape (2-4, diagram C). Cut a hole on the folded edge for the neck. Turn the fabric inside out and attach the head (2-4, diagram D) to the inside of the puppet body. Use masking tape to secure the neck tube.

Variations:

Facial features may be painted on, but the premade circles on thumbtacks and sticky dots yield neat results in an instant. A scarf around the neck is attractive, and hides the point where head, tube, and body meet. If the thumbtacks loosen up, small amounts of glue can be used to secure them. Experiment with hats, beards, moustaches, glasses, funny noses, and different mouths.

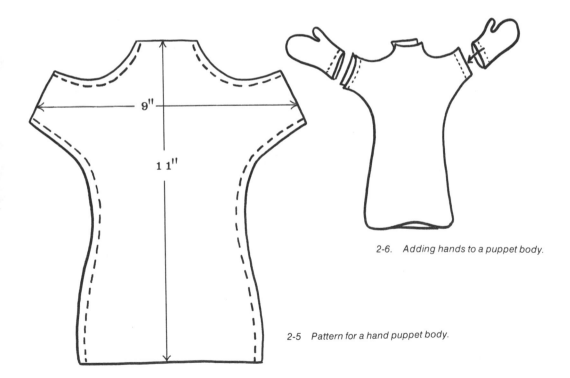

9"

1 1"

2-6.   *Adding hands to a puppet body.*

2-5   *Pattern for a hand puppet body.*

#2. Regular Hand Puppets

Two distinct tasks are involved in the construction of most hand puppets: construction of the head and construction of the body. The body design described here is very basic. Almost all hand puppets have bodies that are only slight variations on this pattern. The dimensions may be changed, of course, but most adults and children will find these dimensions comfortable. I advise that you follow this pattern at least the first time you build a hand puppet. After that, I can't encourage you enough to experiment with your own different methods of body construction.

Constructing the body

Draw the pattern you will cut out to size on the wrong side of the fabric (see 2-5).Tailor's chalk is best, but felt tip pens work well also.

Cut through two thicknesses of fabric. Placing right sides together, sew as indicated by the dotted lines. Turn up a ½-inch wide hem at the bottom.

Turn this garment right side out so that the nice side of the fabric shows on both the front and back. Glue or sew the hands in place, and the puppet body is ready for costuming (2-6). The hands can be sewn fabric, paper maché, sculpted foam rubber, carved wood, or cast latex rubber. You can avoid the labor of making a matched pair of hands by cutting the hands off an old doll, provided that the tips of your fingers will fit inside. Use your imagination and anything that works.

Constructing Puppet Heads

The following materials are excellent for beginning puppet builders: paper maché, plaster-coated gauze, styrofoam, foam rubber, and fabric. Puppet heads can also be made out of celastic, plastic wood, and latex rubber, but these materials are more difficult to work with.

Paper Maché—Kindergarten paper maché is made by soaking strips of paper in water until the fibers break down to form a pulp. Flour is then added as an adhesive. I have had better luck, however, using strips of brown paper towels coated with white glue. These strips, applied in criss-crossing layers, are very strong when they dry.

In order to keep the head light in weight, begin the construction of paper maché head on a frame (such as an old light bulb or a balloon). After a few layers of glued paper strips are dry on the entire surface, the frame underneath can be removed (the balloon is popped; the light bulb can be shattered to remove it). Then a neck tube should be added and the features of the face built up.

Two ready-made paper maché materials are available at most craft shops. One is called Cel-U-Clay, the other, Sculptamold. If you can find them, they are worth trying.

Celastic Substitutes—Because celastic requires acetone as a solvent, it is unsafe for children and requries special room ventilation. Instead, check out your local toy store or art supply shop for one of the numerous craft fabric materials that uses water as a solvent. These become pliable when wet, then become very stiff when the water evaporates.

Drape-It is the commercial name for one such prestarched craft gauze. The plaster-coated gauze products called Plastex and Paris-Craft are similar. All are used like strips of paper maché. Layer upon layer of strips are added to build up the features of the face and head.

Another interesting product is called Dip-It. This polymer solution comes in a jar, and makes any fabric soaked in it as hard as nails. I had particularily nice results using heavyweight craft crepe paper soaked in the Dip-It solution. The crepe paper stretches to cover rounded surfaces easily. It dries in about fifteen minutes, which is nice but requires you to work quickly. When dry, its strength is comparable to celastic.

Styrofoam—Styrofoam (expanded polystyrene) is ideal for the frame of a puppet head. It can be cut, shaped, and dented easily. It is inexpensive and lightweight, and can be glued to other pieces of styrofoam with white glue. (Do not use glue that has a plastic solvent; it will melt the styrofoam.)

To build durable puppet heads out of styrofoam, I advise you to strengthen the surface with any of the celastic substitutes. Don't sculpt the fine details of the face before covering it with the protective strips of gauze. Instead, work the styrofoam into the basic shape of the head and use the protective substance to further your modeling.

Foam Rubber Heads—Most foam rubber is not really rubber at all, but actually polyurethane. This spongey material can be sculpted with a sharp pair of scissors to form puppet heads. Those spherical "Nerf" balls are great for the basic frame. Facial details can be cut out of scraps of foam and glued in place with contact cememt. When the face is fully modeled, spray-paint it a solid color. Finer details, such as pupils, eyelashes, and eyebrows, can be painted on with acrylic paint.

The big drawbacks to foam rubber are that it can rip easily, and that your wonderful creations will rot in time. You can't stop the foam from breaking down, but the less exposure it gets to air and sunlight, the longer it will last.

Fabric Heads—If you are handy with a sewing machine, consider constructing heads entirely of fabric. Experiment with your own patterns (or read Tom Tichenor's *Puppet Book*, which shows in detail how to sew puppet heads).

Fuzzy fabric, fake fur, and terry cloth are good materials for animal characters. Felt is also good, because it can be stretched when wet to partially cover rounded surfaces. Be sure that the dye of the felt is colorfast before throwing the fabric in water.

When designing patterns for cloth puppet heads, try to arrange the seams in the least obtrusive places. Sometimes a seam right down the center of the face is ideal because the nose and eyes will help hide the

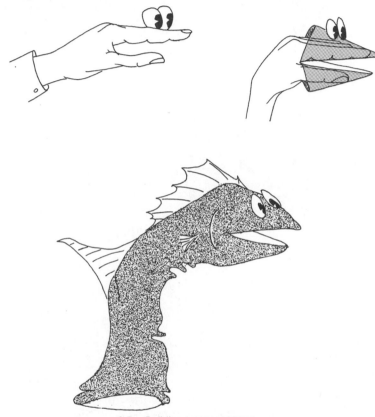

2-7. Building a puppet with an
animated mouth.

seam. Tiny stitches and carefully hidden seams are a must for television puppets that will be seen in extreme close-ups. For most other purposes the seams will not be noticeable—unless, of course, you don't match the color of the thread to the fabric.

#3. *Hand Puppets With Mouths.*

Your goal in designing a puppet with a mouth is to provide a lower jaw, that can be moved in isolation from the rest of the puppet. The top half of the mouth should remain stationary when the puppet speaks to allow you control over the puppet's eye contact. A strong thumb is

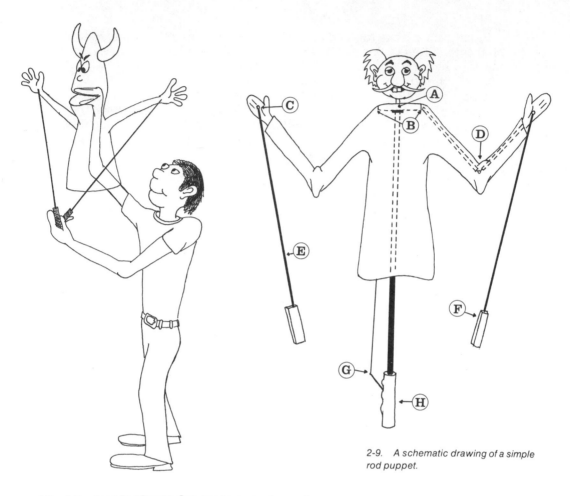

2-9.   A schematic drawing of a simple
rod puppet.

2-8.   A Hand and Rod Puppet. One hand animates the mouth;
the other is free to operate the rods that move the arms.

required for such control, but the design of the puppet is important as
well. The jaw should hang all the way open easily, without any
interference. If a great effort is required to open the mouth, the
puppeteer's hand will become tired too quickly. The puppeteer also
should be able to close the mouth of the puppet completely without a
great deal of effort.

When constructing a puppet with a mouth, build the mouth
mechanism first (2-7). Stiff cardboard hinged with cloth tape works
well for the mouth plates. A sheet of half-inch foam can then be cut
and glued to the cardboard to form the pockets that will keep your
hand in place. Then you can add almost any kind of body or head. The
important thing is that the puppeteer's hand fit snugly but comfortably
in the mouth mechanism. Everything else can be varied, but the

specifications for the mouth mechanism remain constant. Even when the size or shape of the mouth is varied, the design must include pockets on the inside of the mouth to keep the hand flat against the mouth plates. The thumb and fingers should fit into the pocket without any extra space. This snug fit allows the puppeteer the utmost control of the puppet's mouth movements. Loose-fitting puppets can always be stuffed with padding, but there's little that can be done for a puppet that cramps your hand except starting over and rebuidling. It's just good common sense to experiment and find the size that's best for you before you proceed to finish a character.

#4. Hand and Rod Puppet

This sort of puppet has been made very popular in this country by Jim Henson's Muppets on Sesame Street. The puppeteer works with one hand in the head to animate the mouth. The other hand controls the rods; usually one at a time, but two rods may be operated at once (see 2-8).

The head and body do not have to be one piece as illustrated in 2-8. The head would taper to form a sleeve, like a hand puppet; the body would be a separate piece, with a hole for this neck sleeve. Like a turtle, the head is capable of movement independent of the body. The flexible neck extends from within the rigid body, allowing the head to turn and move up and down while the body remains in one position.

If the head and body are one piece, be sure that nothing blocks or gives resistance to the lower jaw. It must be able to fall completely open without straining the puppeteer's thumb.

Because the puppeteer's hand is right in the mouth, it's best to construct these puppets out of a pliable material. Foam rubber or fabric are ideal because they bend and allow the puppeteer to contort the face of the puppet when desired. Puppets with mechanical mouths are not capable of this kind of expressiveness, but the human hand in the mouth of a puppet can create wonderfully subtle facial expressions. Good examples of this technique are Sheri Lewis' Lamb Chop puppet and Jim Henson's Kermit the Frog puppet. Both have cloth faces that bend easily in response to the fingers moving inside. The experienced hand inside really makes the difference, but the material and design of the puppet are very important as well.

Sometimes these puppets have legs and feet that can be operated by another person. You can attach rods to the feet, or wear black gloves and actually grasp the heel of the foot to move it around.

The variations on this basic hand and rod concept are almost limitless. If you plan to experiment with this kind of design, start with the mouth mechanism and add anything else after that. Keep it simple, efficient, lightweight, and durable, and you'll have the makings of a great puppet.

#5. *Basic Rod Puppet.*

Instead of showing you how to build a particular rod puppet, in this section I will cover the general specifications common to all rod puppets as shown in illustration 2-9.

Shoulder Plate (Point A). The body of the puppet is attached to the shoulder plate. If you want the head to turn separately from the body, this plate should not be glued or nailed to the main support rod. Instead, the plate should be supported by a flange just below. Plywood is the best material for the shoulder plate. It can be cut in a circle or oval with a hole in the center.

Arms (Point B). The arms are attached to the shoulder plate at point B. Cloth, leather, eyelets, or rope can be used as a hinge support for the arms. The arms can be metal or wood rods, foam rubber, or fabric sewn into a tube shape and stuffed. 2-9 shows arm rods concealed by the puppet costume. If the arms are out in the open, neatness will count; otherwise, what's underneath the costume does not have to be attractive.

Hands (Point C). The rod controlling the hands is attached at point C. The rod can be permanently embedded in the hand or tied to the outside of the hand or wrist. An eyelet or hole at the end of the hand is necessary if it is to be tied in place.

Elbow Joint (Point D). The same material used as a hinge at the shoulders can be used to hinge the elbow. The elbow should be very flexible, yet engineered so that it does not bend backwards in an unnatural way. A string tether is the most common solution to this problem. If the arms are very light, or if the hands are attached only to the end of the costume sleeve (with no rod inside the arm), you may want to put a weight at the elbow. This will allow gravity to pull the elbow down in a natural way.

Hand Rod (Point E). The hand rod should be as stiff and as thin as possible. Umbrella rods or coat hangers may be adequate, if the hands are not too heavy. If the rod is thin and topheavy, you will have trouble controlling the hands. Welding rods are good, but the best material is spring steel. The hand rods may be painted flat black or the color of the body costume (to blend in when the arm crosses in front of the body). The rods should be long enough for the puppet to reach all the way above his head without the puppeteer's hands showing (longer than illustrated here).

Handles (Point F). Many kinds of handles can be attached to the hand rods. Tape may be wound around the end, or wood or foam may be shaped to form a handle. Good handles allow both puppet arms to be controlled by one puppeteer hand—like chopsticks. Experiment to find what's comfortable for you.

Lever (Point G). A lever with a string attached can be used to control the animation of the head. Moving mouths, eyes, eyebrows, or tilting heads can be operated in this way. Experiment to position the levers comfortably if you want to be able to operate more than one animated feature at a time.

You may want to attach a spring to the lever to keep the line taut at all times. Another possibility is to construct the lever out of springy steel that pulls the string down through its own force. Just be careful that the strength of the spring is only enough to keep the line tight. It shouldn't activate the animation by itself.

Main Support Rod (Point H) The main support rod does not need to have a handle, but you may find one convenient. Sometimes a thin rod is harder to grip and hold than a handle. Finger grips, such as those on bicycle handles, are helpful to keep your hand from sliding. If your puppet has head animation, it is essential that your hand remain in the best position to control the levers.

Very tall rod puppets, such as those found in large scale theatre productions, may be supported with the aid of a stirrup worn around the neck of the puppeteer. In this case there should be no handle on the end. The point of the rod fits into the pocket of the stirrup. With such a device, the puppeteer merely has to balance the puppet; the weight is supported by the neck straps. Honor guardsmen carrying flags on poles use such stirrups to ease their load. You should consider this possibility seriously. Stirrups also help keep the puppet at a constant height. Remember that puppeteers with tired arms have a tendency to let their puppets sink.

Professional Construction Materials

Celastic, latex rubber, and plastic wood are excellent materials from which to build puppets. However, they are expensive and somewhat difficult to work with. Usually only advanced puppet builders use these materials.

Celastic. Celastic is the trade name for a special fabric impregnated with plastic resins. When this fabric comes into contact with acetone thinner it becomes very pliable; but when the acetone evaporates it leaves the fabric rock hard. The object is to get the fabric into the position you desire before the acetone evaporates.

Strips of celastic can be used like paper maché over the basic frame of a puppet head. A lightweight styrofoam frame does not have to be removed, but a clay frame will have to be scraped out when the celastic is dry.

To get at the inside of a dried celastic puppet head, a mat knife can be used to cut the head in half. The clay frame can then be picked out of all the corners and any animation features installed. When you want to put the head together again, a few strips of celastic will patch the seam.

If you'd rather not have to cut open the head to remove pieces of clay, you can construct the frame out of styrofoam. However, since acetone will dissolve styrofoam you must seal the surface before applying the wet celastic strips. Aluminum foil or a layer of paper towels and glue painted with gesso (canvas primer) will adequately protect the styrofoam from the acetone.

Celastic strips can also be laid in a mold for a puppet head. The procedure is almost identical with that used in molding plastic wood.

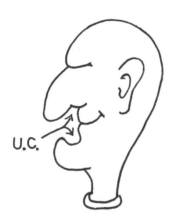

2-10 This clay model cannot be cast in plaster. Note the undercutting.

2-11. Brass strips are stuck into the clay to divide the plaster into the separate mold sections.

Plastic Wood. As its name implies, plastic wood is a putty-like substance that dries to become a material with the workability of real wood. It can be used on top of a frame, but it's most effective when used in a plaster mold.

To make a plaster mold, one must sculpt the desired puppet head in clay. There must be no undercutting, or the head will get stuck in the mold (see 2-10).

Next, thin brass strips are stuck in the clay model (2-11), dividing it into two symmetrical halves. Before applying the plaster, the clay should be painted with tincture of green soap to make removing the clay from the mold easier. The dry plaster should be mixed with water until it has a loose, but not drippy, consistency. The plaster is then literally thrown, in small pieces, on the clay model. Throwing prevents air bubbles from forming. When the entire surface is covered, a thick layer of plaster can be placed on the model to make a strong mold.

When the plaster is completely dry (twenty-four to forty-eight hours) the halves can be separated, the clay removed, and the molds carefully washed clean. The mold is now ready to be used.

Paint the inside surface of the mold with tincture of green soap. Then start applying small pieces of plastic wood, taking care to avoid air bubbles. Coat the entire surface with a thin layer of plastic wood. Allow it to dry before adding another layer for strength. (This same procedure would be used for celastic.) When the two halves are dry, remove them and patch them together with plastic wood. You now have a rough head ready for finishing. You may build up certain features, sand down others, and carve undercutting at this point. The last step is to paint face features and add hair.

If animation mechanisms are going to be added, the work should be done before the finishing touches go on. As with celastic, you may cut the top or back of the head off to get at the inside. If you've made a clean cut, you will not have to use more plastic wood to patch the seam. Instead, plastic wood solvent can be used to glue the sections back together. The ability of plastic wood to be glued back together so neatly with solvent is especially handy if something fouls up inside the head of a finished puppet. Dick Myers told me that even if the puppet is painted, little damage will be done if he has to get at the inside. Any other material would require drastic repair work.

Latex Rubber. Latex rubber is probably the most difficult material to work with. However, it is not without its advantages. Latex rubber puppets are durable, lightweight, and have an amazingly skin-like look, feel, and movement.

The biggest problem in casting latex rubber is that the clay model must be perfect. The procedures for making the plaster cast are identical to those for plastic wood or celastic—the big difference is that what comes out of the mold cannot be worked further.

A flawless clay head is sculpted (no undercutting). All the surfaces must be smooth as silk, because the cast head will look *identical* to the clay model. Any bumps or ripples will show up on your finished product.

The plaster cast is made, the clay is removed, and the two halves of the cast are joined back together.

Liquid latex rubber is poured into the mold and sloshed around inside until the desired thickness has adhered to the walls of the mold.

The excess liquid rubber is poured out and the mold is set aside to let the rubber dry.

Eventually, the mold is opened up and the rubber head is removed. It is then vulcanized in a kiln to give the rubber long life. Without this heat treatment, the rubber would get hard and crack with age.

This method of construction is ideal when duplication is required. This is what I saw at the Bil Baird workshops. They have been able to create hundreds of puppet hands from a single pair of molds by casting multiple latex parts.

If you're intrigued by this construction method, the best way to learn the exact procedure is to study with someone who's mastered the technique. You can experiment on your own, but the initial expense of the equipment and materials is really a problem.

Basic Portable Stages

The majority of puppet stages in this country are portable. But portable is a very broad word, and can mean anything not nailed down. For our purposes, when I say portable I mean *easily* portable.

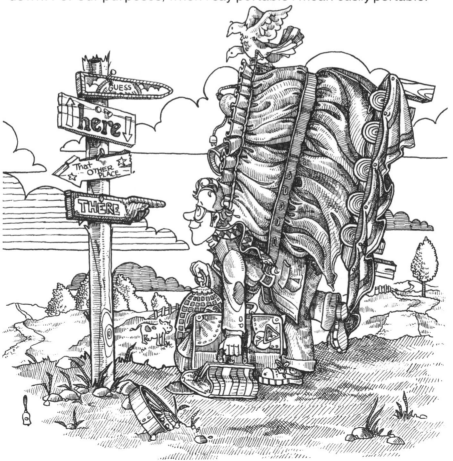

Portable stages are desirable because puppeteers can then pick up and go where the audiences are. An old proverb makes the point: "If the mountain will not come to Mohammed's puppet show, then Mohammed's puppet show will go to the mountain." Of course, today the shortened version of this proverb is more common.

The distance you travel to do a show is limited only by your personal preferences. If you dislike traveling and motels, stick to neighboring counties. If you like life on the road and seeing new areas of the country, consider publicizing your show widely—once you're good enough, that is. A beginning puppet group should start small and try to develop a good reputation in its own community. Still the problems of packing up a show to take it across town, are not very different from those encountered when taking a show across several states.

A real factor that must affect your plans is the type of transportation available. Do you have a van? A station wagon? A pick-up truck? It's just plain handy to know how much weight and volume you can manage *before* you build your show. Shows that travel must do without many nice extras. You should plan to bring only the bare essentials, unless you don't mind moving lots of heavy stuff in and out of a rented truck. You should also keep down the number of vehicles you use, because every additional vehicle will increase your expenses, especially on long trips. Try to allow room inside your vehicle for your staff as well as your equipment.

Just as the early pioneers continually lightened their loads as they gained experience in living off the land, I find myself designing each show and stage far lighter and more compact than the previous one. You too will find yourself trying always to economize further on weight and volume.

Perhaps you know that 90 per cent of your shows will be given in your basement. Still, for the few times you are invited to perform elsewhere, it's nice to have planned ahead. This means building a stage that can travel fairly easily, even though you know it will be used *primarily* in a permanent set-up.

A puppet stage is a place for puppets to perform. The main purpose of a puppet stage is to direct the attention of the audience to the puppets. It does this by masking off areas you don't want the audience to see. It hides the puppeteers, the mess backstage, the lighting equipment, and puppets about to make surprise entrances.

It is important that your stage be sturdy as well as portable. Ideally, your stage design should be a happy compromise between light-as-a-feather and sturdy-as-a-rock. Admittedly these goals are conflicting, but you should keep them both in mind when planning a production and building a show. Another important consideration is set up time. A stage with extensive cross-bracing will undoubtedly be sturdy, but it will also take a long time to set up (and every extra piece of support adds bulk and weight).

Keep in mind that any stage that works efficiently is fine. Choosing the ideal stage depends on your situation, needs, and personal tastes—and the type of puppet that will perform on it.

I have not included any blueprints for puppet stages here because there are already enough repetitions of the same old designs. Rather

2-12.   The basic wall.

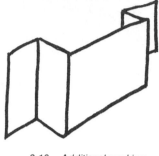

2-13.   Additional masking.

these examples illustrate various approaches to the problem, and point out their advantages and disadvantages. If you find features that you like in one or several approaches, experiment to develop a new approach to the classic problem of hiding the puppeteers and presenting the puppets. If you'd rather work from a blueprint, these appear in many puppetry books and in back issues of *The Puppetry Journal*.

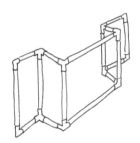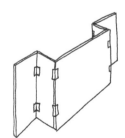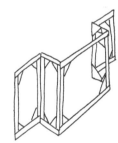

2-14.   Constructing the basic frame.

A puppet stage hides the puppeteer. So, let's start with the idea of a wall (2-12). The puppeteers will be on one side of the wall and the audience will be on the other. But what about people sitting on the far sides who can see around the wall? Obviously, some additional masking is needed (2-13).

This is a good start. Now depending on the material from which the frame is made, additional plans can be made (2-14). Fabric is ideal to cover these frames. You may use plain white canvas and paint a design on it, or a colored fabric. Whatever is used should be light tight. Thin fabrics will have to be doubled or lined. Heavy fabrics may not

need lining, but be sure that the audience will not see any light
through them.

Now, let's consider the most important thing. For what kind of
puppets are you designing a stage? Marionettes will need a
proscenium opening down below. Hand puppets or rod puppets can
use a proscenium opening, or they can play above the stage wall with
or without a proscenium opening.

2-15.   Using hand or rod puppets on a stage.

Puppeteers can use hand or rod puppets on the stage in four ways
(2-15). Note that each of these walls has a rectangle on top
representing the playboard. The playboard should be about six inches
wide, three-quarters inch thick, and the length of the front of your
stage. The playboard is necessary to put props and scene pieces on.

The height of the playboard from the ground depends on the height
of the puppeteers, and whether they will sit or stand. In all but one
of these setups (2-15), the puppeteers are below the puppets looking
up. The scenery in these arrangements can be opaque, or cut out to
reveal another row of scenery or the rear wall. If you design scenery on
a scrim (gauze like) material, the puppeteers can see through it; with
proper lighting the audience will not see the puppeteers. All the light
must come from the audience side of the scrim. If the puppeteers are
in darkness only the design painted on the scrim will be visible to the
audience. Note that the scenery scrim must be close to the playboard
in order to allow the puppeteer to reach the playboard with the
puppet.

Marionette Stages

Because the proscenium opening on a marionette stage is low, it is a good idea to set the entire stage up on risers or tables. This way, your entire audience should be able to see the show. Otherwise, only the first row of people would have an unobstructed view.

2-16.   A marionette stage.

Marionette operators have two options when they construct a stage. The first is simply to stand on the same level of the puppets; using a backdrop of some sort keeps the audience from seeing the puppeteer's legs (2-16). The second is to place the puppeteers up on a bridge. (The puppets then must have longer strings.) The advantage to a bridge is that it takes the puppeteers out of the backstage area, leaving more depth for the scenery. You can even have more than one bridge, allowing yet greater depth to the playing area.

Commonly, bridges are constructed with railings for the puppeteers to lean over when they are operating the marionettes. The brave, however, may dispense with railings. The Bil Baird Theatre uses two parallel bridges without railings. The bridges are only about 2½ feet apart, and the puppets are operated in the space between them. The puppeteers can step back and forth between the two bridges freely because there are no railings to obstruct them. This helps immensely when characters are required to walk in opposite directions past each other. Oridinarily, puppeteers on one bridge would get rather contorted passing each other; with this arrangement, the puppeteers merely stand on separate bridges. There is an element of danger in working without a railing, but Bil maintains that he has fallen off only once in his entire career.

Professional Puppet Theatres

The Bil Baird Theatre is run by the American Puppet Arts Council, a non-profit organization. The theatre is housed in a six-story building at 59 Barrow Street, New York City, 10014. It contains workshops, a rehearsal stage, Bil's home, and more than 3,000 puppets in storage.

Since its opening (Christmas Day, 1966) more than 1,500 performances have been given. The repetoire includes; *Winnie the Pooh, The Wizard of Oz, Davy Jones Locker, Pinocchio, People is the Thing the World is Fullest of, Ali Baba and the Forty Thieves, The Whistling Wizard and The Sultan of Tuffet, Peter and The Wolf,* and *Bil Baird's Bandwagon.*

Although a good deal of support is obtained from tickets sold for the 194 seat house, the theatre requires substantial public and private assistance to function. This assistance is received primarily from National Endowment for the Arts, Andrew H. Mellon, The John Golden Fund, Billy Rose, Mary Reynolds Babcock, Rockefeller, William C. Whitney, Heckscher, Jean Tennyson, Marion Ascoli; Foundations and The New York Foundation.

The following conversation took place between Bil Baird and myself on January 17, 1975, in the house on Barrow Street:

Would you please tell me about the permanent stage at the Bil Baird Theatre?
Permanent stages, of course, depend on a permanent audience. If you're lucky and you've got a permanent audience, it's a great thing. This is our ninth year in this permanent stage theatre—and still in order to really make it work we have to go out and tour. So I have a permanent stage here, twenty-four feet wide with three openings in it. My touring stage has exactly the same opening dimensions, but is thirty-six feet wide overall.

Now this touring stage has been a very useful stage. We've been all over India and Russia with it, and we've been quite a bit all over America. We've got so that we can set it up in about two hours and tear it down in an hour and a half. We sometimes do two shows a day with this stage, and we also carry a small three-man hand puppet stage, which goes up in about twenty minutes.

When you design a show that's going to tour, are you really conscious of limitations?
Absolutely. For instance, we did *Pinocchio* last year. On my permanent stage we have a marionette floor that moves upstage and allows us a pit for hand puppets and rod puppets. Within seconds we can use rod puppets and hand puppets, in the same show, in the same opening. Or, we can run hand puppets and marionettes in the same opening, at the same time, just by cracking the stage a little bit. That's very successful.

When we go on the road, I don't have that same facility, because we don't have a pit. Our stage floor is twenty inches off the ground. A traveling hand puppet or rod puppet stage is nowhere near as complicated as a marionette stage. But, we started out with marionettes, and we've made it work both ways. Our *Pinocchio* has to be changed just a little bit to play on the road, but we have two hand puppet stages, one on either side, which help quite a bit. We have to change the looks of the play just a little bit, but it works.

You turn a marionette show into a rod puppet show?
No, no, to do the same things. We are a combo anyhow. I do strings and rods all the time together.

*Oh, so you're saying you have to change the blocking of the show a little
bit to get it out on the road.*
    Yes, just change the look of it. Sometimes we have to move some of
the stuff that usually plays center stage to one of the side stages.

*Is it really that hard to allow for a pit in the stage you take on the
road?*   Well, when we went out to California to open the Stanford
Festival a couple of years ago, we raised our stage up thirty-three
inches higher than the twenty inches it is now. This gave us a pit to
operate in—not standing, but on stools.

What show was that?
    We were playing *Davey Jones* and *People Is*—which is strictly an
adult show. But it just proved too dangerous to have puppeteers way
up that high on the bridge. We added to the length of our ladders and
everything, which threw it up in the air. I suppose on a permanent
structure, where you can brace in all directions, it would be all right
but I just wasn't able to make our thing sturdy enough. However, we
did it.

This was to play to how large an audience?
    Two thousand; in the big theatre there at Stanford. We often play to
audiences like that. We've toured a good deal and our aluminium
traveling stage has proved a very successful stage. When we toured
Davey Jones with it, I couldn't have asked for anything better.

Do you go out on all the road shows?
    I used to, but I haven't lately. These younger people who are
working for me now are stronger, and they can take it better.

How many stages do you have?
    I have about twelve stages here.

Twelve touring stages?
    No, I have a permanent movie stage here for shooting television
commercials and films. Then I have one to use in a television studio
theatre—playing the Ed Sullivan Show, for instance. I have one that
we used with Kostelanetz up at Lincoln Center, and we have other
ones for doing outdoor shows. For instance, when we went to India we
took an outdoor rod puppet stage that is about twenty-four feet wide
in the background and twelve feet in the enclousure where we do the
puppets.

*I remember a picture from your book showing a marionette operator
leaning over the back wall. Is that how you did your show?*
    Yes, we did a little bit of everything. Mostly it was just rods.

With the operator hidden?
  That's right, but we demonstrated strings for just a little bit.

They had never seen string puppets before?
  Yes they had, but not like ours.

This was in what part of the country?
  This was in Nepal. As a matter of fact, they weren't sure that the puppets weren't alive in Nepal.
  Stages are the most important thing you need to give a show. For instance, we gave a show in Hyderabad and the local puppet company, which is a Rajasthan marionette company, wanted to give us a show. Well, they waited around and after three days they came up and put a thing on right in front of our stage. I just gave them an old drape and loaned them our base drum, and they put on the show right in front of us.
  My stages are all just different things we need to play in different places. It's a shame that you have to tote so much stuff around sometimes.
What would you say about priorities for someone in this country who wants to build a stage? If they're worried about the bulk and weight, but want something that will be sturdy and at the same time set up fast, what advice do you have?
  It all depends on the show. What kind of show do you have? Make your stage to fit the show and the number of people you have to perform it but make it as simple as possible. You must hide your operators and bring out your puppets to the best advantage. For a marionette stage, I've found aluminium best by far: aluminium is light and goes up in a hurry. Stay away from bolts with wing nuts that have to be turned, because turning them takes time. If you can just run a thing into a slot and give it a quarter turn you're very much time ahead. Each problem is separate. I've designed perhaps 100 stages. For Radio City Music Hall I had special stages, and for the Roxy theatre, I had special stages. One time we played in the Ruban Bleu, and my traveling stage was a foot too wide. I had to make another stage in a hurry—a foot narrower.

You sometimes work in full view of the audience don't you?
  Oh sure. In the Ziegfeld Follies we operated right on a little platform, about eighteen inches high with a circular front six feet wide. We were in full dress, in full view of the audience, and the lighting director just spotted the puppets. That was it. We had about six or seven minutes to do. The puppets were there, and we were there, and the people were conscious of us—but we weren't important because the puppets were important. It was a big huge spotlight, from the top of the Winter Garden Theatre. We'd wheel the platform out, I'd let down the front,

and we were on in something like eleven seconds. Behind us was a black curtain, about five feet high, hiding the puppets hanging up. I'd bring the puppets through the center, through a little gate, and operate. Now, that's a nightclub stage.

Do you like playing in nightclubs?
    Well, I've played in nightclubs where they've resented the fact that our stage took up so much space. It took up the space of a couple of small tables at which people might have been eating. So, sometimes the waiters would spill spaghetti on the puppets—but that was because we were playing in a nightclub. Last summer I did the Johnny Carson Show, and we brought out a simple stage that's only about four feet wide and five feet high.

For what kind of puppets?
    Hand puppets. Then I did another number on a little platform they built for me.

Would you say, that generally, you always try to economize on weight and bulk when you design a stage?
    Yes, of course—but it depends on what the show is. I've taken our full big stage and used it on the Ed Sullivan Show. We just put it on wheels, ran it out into place, and did a number from *Davey Jones*. I don't like to get too big, but when we play Lincoln Center we use a stage thirty-five to fourty feet wide: just something to hide us and a six-inch deep playboard.

How do you cover your sightlines for people way up in the balcony when a theatre is steeply raked?
    Well, we were playing in back of the orchestra and they put us up three feet high.

And the people up in the balcony couldn't see your heads?
    A little bit—but we all wear black hoods and the audience is more interested in the show. If the show's any good they're not going to think about the operators. For instance, people sometimes ask how we hide the strings. I say if the show is any good you don't notice the strings.

Are most of your productions pre-recorded on tape?
    No, just the music.

You mike the operators?
    For speech. When I did *The Dragon and the Dentist* last summer, I put it all on tape. The three operators have to work so fast in that show that I can't get them close to microphones. If I had lavalieres on them

they'd get all tangled up. But ordinarily we have mikes hanging over the operators. It works. You see, if you're playing to an audience you want to get a reaction. A musical play is different. If it's all music I tape it; but if it's something you're playing for laughs, you have to mike it.

I remember you saying that if there was one thing you could redesign in your theatre, you would try to get an extra hundred seats. Is there anything else that you would change?
Yes, I'd like to have a little more depth so that we could use rear-projected scenery sometimes. I'd like to have a little more side space, too, so that we could have more stuff. We're very limited in scenery here, because there's no place to put it except to fly it. I do have a good set of flies, though. The stage is two stories high. But really every inch backstage is accounted for; there's somebody in it. If we have eight or nine people backstage, that's a lot of people.

I take it that these are not big enough problems to make you consider moving?
How could I move now? That would just be impossible. This is a great place as far as getting an audience. We're right near the subway and we're situated well in town. I bought the building fifteen years ago. It would be impossible to find anything else, at this time, anywhere near the price I paid for this one.

Is is possible to expand next door?
No, there's no place I could go. We're right up against the other buildings. This isn't an ideal place for a theatre, but it is an ideal place for all the different things that I do. To really get a theatre, the city would have to revamp an old one for me—but even then, I couldn't afford to keep it dark. With this one, if I'm dark for a few months each year it doesn't kill me. No, with real estate the way it is now any other arrangement would be practically impossible. Of course, if I were to go to some school—a college, or something like that—there would be no problem. Except that, there wouldn't be an audience. I mean you might be able to play in a population center two or three months out of the year, but then you'd have played to them.

So you think that being situated in New York City is really an important factor in surviving as a permanent theatre?
I do think so. But still this theatre doesn't make money. If it wasn't for touring and grants and things like that, we just couldn't make it. Of course, we do have the movies and other things that we do here. And it's very nice that I don't have to commute. I just slide down the bannister and I'm at work.

THE HEAD IS HELD AS HIGH OVER MY HEAD AS I CAN MANAGE.

YES, MY ARM FEELS LIKE IT MIGHT ACHE RIGHT OFF, BUT THATS PART OF PUPPETRY TIDDLETYPOM!

INSIDE, I WEAR A TINY 1½" TV MONITOR AND MICROPHONE IT HELPS IMMENSELY!

THE RIGHT WING IS RUN LIKE A MARIONETTE —ON A STRING FROM MY LEFT ARM.

BIG BIRD STANDS OVER EIGHT FEET TALL!

5" HEELS INSIDE THE FEET TO MAKE ME TALLER!

In this illustration, drawn by Carol Spinney, he relates how he operates Big Bird's head with one hand and the wing with another. A wireless microphone and a television monitor are strapped to his chest. This enables Mr. Spinney to see Big Bird's movements from the audience point of view. The initial idea for Big Bird was sketched by Jim Henson, and then built by Kermit Love. The mechanics of the head were designed and built by Don Sahlin.

Illustration courtesy Carol Spinney

The motion of Big Bird's wings is controlled by the arm in the left wing. A thin wire runs from the stuffed right wing, up to Big Bird's neck, and down to the left wing (the wire is partially visible in the photo). Moving the left wing up causes the right wing to go down, and vice-versa. Standing next to the giant Muppet are Susan (Loretta Long) and Bob (Bob McGrath), two of Sesame Street's original hosts.
Courtesy Children's Television
Workshop

The Gingerbread House. This outdoor puppet trailer is used to present gospel puppet shows and anti-drug puppet shows. The One-Way Puppets of Pompano Beach, Florida, is an outreach of the Turning Point Ministries. Courtesy Bob Dolan, Pompano Beach,

These puppets are from a production entitled Fiesta Mexicana. The show toured Mexico in the fall of 73, and then the United States. Note the stage frame is made of aluminum tubing and requries sandbags stability.

Fabric Puppets by C.A. McCord. Courtesy C.A. McCord-The TangleWood Puppet Theatre, Brentwood, Tenn.

Hand & rod frogs by Phil Morrison of Northridge, California. Note that the arm rods are from discarded umbrellas. This is handy because the eyelet on the end of the rod can be used when sewing the rod to the puppet's wrist.
Photo by Sidney Lee, courtesy Phil Morrison

Pinocchio and Mrs. Bluestone, from
the Bill Baird's Marionettes production
of Pinocchio.
Photo by Nat Messik, courtesy Frank Rowley.

Pinocchio and Geppetto, rod
puppets from the Smithsoniam Puppet
Theatre. These characters were built by
Alan Stevens from an excellent
combination of celastic, plastic, wood,
and fabric.
Photo by Mark Kinnaman,
Courtesy Alan Stevens, Washington, DC.

Here's an ideally portable stage, by
"Puppet Man" Steve Hansen. He can
watch the faces of his audience through
the burlap sack and improvise to their
reactions. His Punch and Judy show is
the best street theatre in the United
States today. Courtesy Steve Hansen, NYC.

Fred Jackson and Bruce Chesse in
action behind a stage wall, using only
available light and no scenery. Note that
two mikes have been taped to the wood
to amplify the voices of the puppeteers.
Courtesy Bruce Chesse

Chapter 3

The Production

When planning the production of a puppet show, it is important to remember that no one element of the show can be planned without considering all the other elements. Each part is dependent on the others. If you keep this in mind, you will be well on your way to a unified professional production.

The puppets and the puppet stage are the first two elements of a puppet production. The others are scenery, props, lighting, sound, music, and script. Each of these elements requires relatively equal consideration. What good is beautiful scenery that is poorly lit—or beautiful lighting on an ugly set? Unfortunately people tend to focus on the weaknesses of your production more easily than it merits. You may have a top notch-show in many respects—but if the fidelity of the sound is poor, that will make the biggest impression on your audience. Therefore, give creative time, thought, money, and energy, more or less equally to *all* the aspects of the production. Do not sacrifice quality in one element in order to put special effort into another. This does not mean that you may not design a show in which for instance, the lighting plays a particularly important role. But make sure that *every* basic element is considered and provided for before giving extra special attention to any one.

Although technical perfection is desirable, nothing can make up for bad puppet manipulation, bad acting, or a bad script. Also, don't forget that sloppy and thoughtless staging can destroy a good script, performed well by competent puppeteers.

Much of this chapter is written with the assumption that you are the director, and that you will be leading a group of people in producing an elaborate puppet production. Admittedly, this may not be your situation. But the considerations and options available to you are similar, even if you are planning a small-scale puppet show. Regardless of the size, remember that it takes enlightened people, enthusiastic about what they're doing, to make the script, puppets, and the production as a whole come to life.

Scenery

The main purpose of scenery in any theatre is to enhance the actors. The fact that you are using puppets makes no difference—they are actors too. Properly designed scenery should not call attention to itself. Good scenery is rarely even noticed. If too little or too much attention is given to the scenery the audience will be distracted from the action of the play.

You may even decide that scenery is not appropriate for your production. Think about this possibility at the beginning, when the script is being written. If your story has a large number of locations, you might want to do without scenery altogether. Or possibly the theme, mood, or style of the play is better suited to an empty, undecorated set. As the director of the production, you must make this choice. But remember that if you choose to do a production without scenery, the burden placed on your lighting will be much greater.

Designing Scenery

In live theatre, scene designers must be equipped to render a wide variety of styles and periods. Realistic, true-to-the-era scenery is not a concern in puppet productions, however, which take place in the realm of fantasy. Stylized scenery, a caricature or exaggeration of the real world works best. But always remember: *The purpose of your scenery is to provide a background for the puppets.* Don't treat the puppet production as an opportunity to show off your graphic art skills. Save them for your publicity posters and programs.

Specifications

As a designer of scenery for a puppet production, you may express yourself in whatever style pleases you. There are, however, certain inflexible criteria your scenery must meet. As long as you keep these in mind, you may do whatever you like in terms of the materials you use or the approach you take to create the scenery.

High on your list of important considerations should be the sightlines of the audience. This is particularly important if the stage

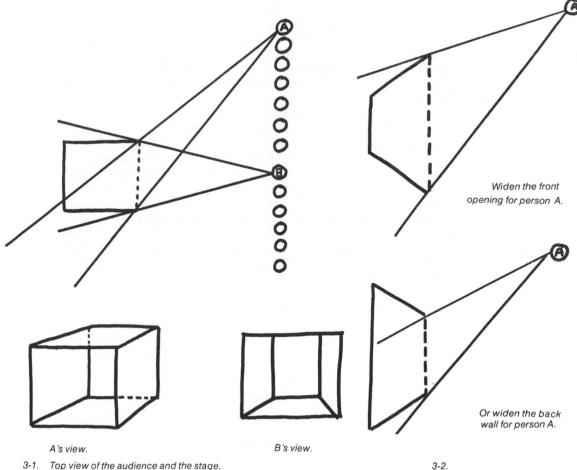

Widen the front opening for person A.

Or widen the back wall for person A.

A's view.

B's view.

3-1. *Top view of the audience and the stage.*

3-2.

has a proscenium arch, as do most marionette stages. A proscenium arch makes the stage into a box, cutting the sightlines drastically. The danger with such a stage is that if the back wall (upstage) is deep, persons not in the center of the audience will see only a small portion of the back wall (3-1). Note the difference between the vantage points of person A and person B).

There are two ways to correct this situation: 1) widen the front opening of the proscenium; 2) widen the back wall of the stage. In either case, you have turned the box (or cube) into a paralelogram (3-2).

The first solution is preferred, since person A can now see the entire acting space; hence no puppets can be hidden from sight, as might happen if the back wall were widened.

Sightline problems are always unique to the stage used and its relationship to the area in which the audience will be seated. It's often hard to give every seat a perfect view—but at least be conscious of the problem. Try to design your scenery so that most of the audience can see scenery behind the puppets.

The type, size, and color of the puppets in your production should also influence your set designs. Scenery has only a supporting role. Choose colors in light, pastel shades; intensely bright and loud colors will compete with the puppets for attention. Try to scale the set design to the size of the puppets. The only time the puppets should be dwarfed by the scenery is at the Giant's house in *Jack and the Beanstalk*. Objects off in the distance should be smaller than those that are close, but remember that tiny details can't be seen by the audience. It's best to work with bold, general outlines. Remember: Keep it simple. The engineering of your scenery mechanism is a vital consideration. How are you planning to keep the scenery in place? Cut-out set pieces can be taped to the backdrop, but then it will take time to change to a new setting. You also run the risk of having the pieces fall down during the show if the tape gives out. If you are using only one set for the entire show, this method is fine, but plan to use a lot of tape, and expect some difficulty removing the pieces (usually several pieces of tape remain on the background when you pull down the cut-outs).

Scenery can be constructed with hooks which attach to the top of the back wall—or string can be attached to the scenery and it can hang. Clothespins or clamps can also be used to fasten scenery from either above or below, provided that you have something strong and sturdy to clamp to. This method allows quick removal and set-up of set pieces.

You might like to experiment with painting the entire scene on a flat surface that can be put into place quickly. Or, a series of window shades can be set up, one behind the other. As each scene is finished, a slight tug on the bottom will wind the shade up, revealing the scene behind it.

Venetian blinds can also be used. Paint your scene on a large piece of paper; then cut it into strips and attach the strips to the blinds. Each side can be used for a different scene. The entire blind can then be raised to reveal another one behind.

Long rolls of fabric or paper can also be used mounted on rollers top and bottom or at the sides. Each new scene is advanced into position by turning the rollers.

Materials

You can use almost anything to construct scenery, provided it is not too heavy. Lightweight materials are best. They won't strain your stage, and will be easier to transport if your show is headed for the road. Beware of fragile materials. Durability is an important factor if you plan to perform your show many times.

Tempera paint, acrylic paint, oil art crayons, and regular latex house paint are all suitable for painted scenery. Choose whatever you have available, or whatever you feel works most easily on the surface to which it is being applied.

If you plan on cut-out silhouettes or semi-three-dimensional scenery, try plywood, masonite, or formica, cut with a jig-saw; heavy cardboard, upson board, or styrofoam board, cut with a mat knife; paper maché or celastic; or corrugated cardboard with muslin glued to it.

Plain corrugated cardboard is undesireable for scenery, because the lines of corrugation are always showing through the paint. Also, it is easily bent and ruined. However, it can be used very successfully in this manner: reinforce it by gluing two sheets together, with the grain's crossing at right angles. Then cut out the pattern desired and glue muslin or canvas to the visible surfaces. The muslin can then be painted without fear of those lines showing through. Use any white glue to adhere the fabric to the cardboard. Be sure to allow for fabric shrinkage during drying. Experiment until you know how much fabric is required to keep the cardboard from curling. This method constructs ideal scenery in terms of durability, light weight, low cost, and ease of construction.

Consider how your scenery will be stored and/or shipped. It should be protected from dust, moisture, sunlight, curious hands, and breakage. Naturally, the more compact it can become, the easier it will be to handle. Flats that can be rolled up are great in this respect.

If your scene changes seem to take a long time (more than fifteen seconds), examine your methods to see if you're using real economy of motion. Rehearse the scene change to see if you can slim down the time. Otherwise, you may have to turn the scene change into a part of the show. Either a puppet or stage hands can be used to change the scenery in full view of the audience. With a little music and mysterious lighting, scene changes can be quite entertaining. Audiences love being involved in the magic of the theatre mechanism. Play it up for what it's worth—but be careful not to destroy the illusion of puppet reality by the frequent interference of human beings.

Projected Scenery. If you can get complete darkness in the area in which you perform your show, you might like to experiment with projected scenery. As with shadow puppets, the light source for the projection comes from behind a screen. Slide, movie, overhead, or opaque projectors can be used. If you have this equipment at your disposal, experiment with using more than one method at a time. Any gauzy material or thin paper can be used as a rear-projection screen. Stretch the screen tightly to avoid wrinkles that could distort your projected image. Control your lighting, carefully so that a minimum spills on the screen. Otherwise, the projected image will be partially or entirely washed out.

Remember: when designing scenery, consider your stage, the audience, and the sightline problems you will encounter. Consider the lighting available, the puppets being used, the story being told, the materials available, and your own artistic talent. Furthermore, take your budget and the time available into account. Above all: *keep it simple.*

Props

Props can be a very nice addition to a puppet production when properly handled. But nothing destroys the illusion of puppet reality more easily than props that fight the puppet. Without adequate consideration of the steps necessary to guarantee flawless manipulation, props can be the worst addition to a puppet production. The trick is to ensure proper handling.

Again, the approach to the problem of props must depend on the particular puppets. Props for a marionette show can be supported by strings of their own. This method is great for magical scenes, in which the objects may begin to fly around. But marionettes have difficulty holding on to most props. It helps to put the prop string through a hole or hook on the hand, or to securely fasten the prop to the hand. Marionettes and rod puppets often have removable hands. When the character has to hold a sword or shield, a new hand—with the prop permanently attached—is snapped into place. This must be set up offstage, however; the puppet can't pick up or put down the prop while on stage.

Muppet-type puppets, which use the puppeteer's real hand, can control large and small props with little difficulty. Remember: if both the puppet's hands are required to handle a prop, it will take two puppeteers. One puppeteer controls the head and one hand; the second puppeteer controls the remaining hand. It takes practice, but coordination between the two hands isn't as hard as you might think. If your show absolutely requires a lot of props, the Muppet-type puppet is without question the best.

Don't forget that props aren't always in the hands of puppets. Sometimes they are required to stay in one place, without falling down or off the playboard. Small pieces of Velcro can be a big help here. (Velcro is that material that comes in two parts: one part is fuzzy, and the other has little barbs. When pressed together, the two parts hold together quite strongly; when desired, they can be separated by a sharp tug. If you've never seen Velcro, take a trip to a sewing supply center and ask to see some.)

Velcro is relatively expensive. A one-inch wide strip costs about a dollar per foot. But if cost is no object, try this (as far as I know, no one's done it yet): cover the entire surface of your playboard with strips of Velcro (use the fuzzy side, because the barb side has a tendency to pick up lint, which hampers it's effectiveness). Next, fasten pieces of the barb strips to the base of all your props. When you put the props on the playboard, you will never have to fear their falling off. Just be careful to keep the Velcro clean, and it will serve indefinitely.

Another possibility is to use magnets. A metalic playboard would give similiar results if all the props contained small magnets in their bases. The noise factor of magnets on a metallic playboard is the only drawback. However, if you know where to get quantities of rubberized magnets, this method might even surpass Velcro.

A third method is the use of felt and sandpaper. This is not nearly so sticky, but large-grain sandpaper does provide good friction when placed against felt—and it's cheap.

I have tried various kinds of tape, with generally poor results. In a pinch, however, if you must use tape, don't rely on cellophane or masking tape. Instead, buy a big roll of duct tape. This is a grey cloth tape that is very sticky. It is similiar to the permasilk gaffer's tape used in the film industry. These large rolls always come in handy during a puppet show, whether for quick repairs or for taping down electric cords. Gaffer's tape is usually one of the first things on my check list. Unfortunately, it is so sticky that it can't be removed without damaging paper and similiar materials.

Hand puppets are good prop handlers. Make sure that the props are three-dimensional. Flat cut-out pieces of paper or cardboard can't be held as easily as thicker objects. As a safety precaution, it's a good idea to tie fishing line to all props that hand puppets will handle. Fasten the other end backstage, just below the playboard. If the puppet drops the prop, it can be retrieved without the puppeteer having to bend over and hunt for it. If a prop falls off the playboard into the audience, you'll be very happy to have it tethered by a string. Otherwise, you run the risk of having it thrown back, or broken, or both. Worst of all, the momentum of your show would be broken. Instead the puppet can pull the string and hoist the prop back up, while you ad-lib your way through. Hopefully the audience will think its part of the show.

Props for rod puppets, naturally enough, should be on rods. The puppeteer grasps the hand rod and the prop rod together, and the prop will appear to be in the hand of the puppet. If the prop is to be set down on the playboard, the rod must be attached to the *back side* of the prop. The rod then can extend down below the backstage side of the playboard. If the rod is in the middle of the prop's base, only an edge of the prop can be set down on the playboard.

Because a rod on the side of a lightweight prop will throw off the center of gravity, it's a good idea to put a small fishing weight in the front side of the prop. That way it will sit flat on the playboard (3-3).

If the prop is heavy it may sit flat by itself, but beware! The weight can make the rod top-heavy and cause it to sway. Try to hollow out such props, or use a thick rod to support them.

As with scenery, simplicity of design is an extremely important quality for props. The features should be large (exaggerated if need be) and clear to people in the back row of the audience. If the prop requires lettering, make it large and preferably white. White letters on a dark background are the most legible.

If the prop must be tiny (for example, a house-fly in the room), try to use day-glow colors to help visibility. Note, however, that large props painted with day-glow paint will compete with the puppets for attention.

When selecting or building props, remember the suggestions already discussed:
1. Props should be lightweight;
2. Props can be supported by strings or rods;
3. A string tether is a good safety feature for loose props;
4. Velcro or magnets are better than tape;
5. Three-dimensional props can be handled more easily by puppets than one-dimensional props;
6. Simplicity and clarity are important design factors.

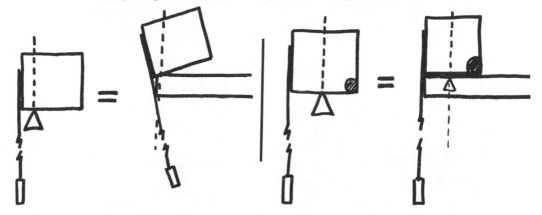

3-3. *Without a weight, the prop is off balance.*   *With a weight, the pull of gravity is balanced.*

Keeping in mind these points, you can use the same materials you would use for making puppets and scenery: balsa wood, styrofoam, celastic, pre-starched or plasterized craft fabrics, homemade paper maché or paper maché-type craft materials, cardboard (with glued on fabric cover), and polyurethane foam. Plaster, wood, bricks, clay, or lead bars are definitely out!

Before you begin a puppet production, make sure all your props are present. A checklist is advisable. It's also handy to have repair materials available, in case something breaks. I always keep an electric glue gun plugged in during a performance. It dispenses molten plastic, which acts like glue when it cools down. Though not nearly as strong as real glue, but it bonds in fifteen seconds—which is extremely handy in an emregency. You must take a pessimistic attitude. Assume that everything that can possibly go wrong will do so. Be prepared was the motto the Boy Scouts tattooed on the inside of my brain, and it really does make sense in a puppet production.

Take the time to store your props carefully. If they have to travel, be sure to make provisions so they won't get damaged. This may sound trivial, but if it's forgotten you'll have broken props when you want to start your play.

Lighting

Lighting is one creative aspect of a puppet production that often is overlooked. Just as scenery provides atmosphere for the play, so does lighting. The key is variety, which can be provided without sophisticated equipment if you use a little imagination.

The chief function of the lights is to illuminate the puppets so that your audience can see them. If your performance is held outdoors during the day, there is little you can do without high wattage instruments. If your performance is indoors, try to set up the hall to provide the greatest degree of darkness. Ideally, with the house lights off, the hall should be completely black. Be sure to tell your sponsors this if you take your show on the road. Maybe they'll be able to find you a location other than a gymnasium with skylights and no curtains. If sunlight shines into the hall even after your best efforts to block it out, you're going to have to live with it. Try to position your stage along the darkest wall, so that no light is coming from behind you. Otherwise, the movement of persons backstage will be apparent through any cracks in or under your stage.

One important lighting effect is the blackout, produced by shutting off all the stage lights at once. It is much more effective if the entire audience is in darkness when the stage lights go off. One precaution, though: don't leave your audience in complete darkness longer than five seconds. The adults will become restless, and may think something has gone wrong. The children will become scared; worst of all, a child may start crying.

The blackout usually comes at the end of a scene or act. Timing is extremely important, especially when you are ending on the last note of a song or the last word of a sentence. If you jump the gun by even a second, the audience will be painfully aware of it. A late cue will make your production look sloppy. With just a little effort here you can impress the audience with a tight professional production, but to achieve this whoever controls your lights must be completely familiar with the show and must attend all your rehearsals.

At the beginning of your show, as the house lights start to go dim, your stage lights should start to come on. If the house lights are not on a dimmer, your stage lights should come on before the house lights are shut off. The idea is to make a gradual transition. (This way, you also check that your stage lights are working before the audience is left in total blackness).

I am not particularly fond of a long musical overture at the beginning of the show, during which the audience sits in darkness. Though this is supposed to create a mood and prepare the audience for the experience to come, I think something to look at is much more effective. Dim lights, candles, fireflies, abstract light patterns, scenery being set up, human hands—you name it. However you handle it, keep the overture relatively short. The actual length would depend on the audience, and on visual experience being presented, but keep in mind that you can easily overdo it and bore your audience.

Lighting Equipment

The most common stage lights are shown in Diagram 3-4, mounted in a Japanese Screen puppet booth. This hypothetical stage is loaded with about twice as many instruments as would be needed at any one time. However, the variety of lighting made possible by different combinations of this equipment would be ideal.

Without front or foot lights, puppets can easily cast shadows on their own face when leaning over the playboard. The slightest tilt towards the audience would obscure the lights on the backstage side of the booth. For this reason, either front or foot lights are essential.

Foot lights should have shields so they don't shine in the eyes of the audience. A trouble light sawed in half will yield an ideal metal shell,

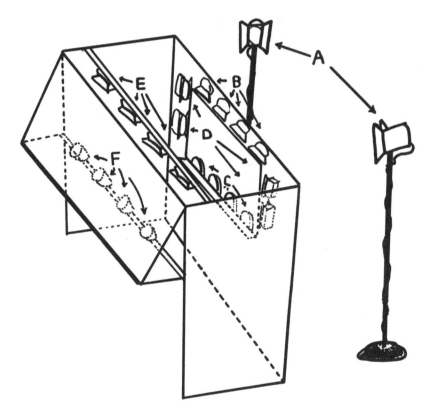

3-4.   *Stage Lighting.*

heat resistant. If you don't want the audience looking at a row of shinny metal footlight shells, spray paint them with black bar-b-que grill paint. Most other paints will not stand the heat.

The front lights should have reflector spot bulbs. These cast a somewhat narrow beam of intense light. The object is to limit the spillage on the stage booth. If you can get instruments with lenses or barn-doors (moveable blinders to control the spillage), all the better.

The main lights fill in from above what is missed from the front. They are aimed at the main acting area.

The back lights are aimed down at the scenery to wash out any shadows the puppets might create. They also provide some back light for the puppets, which is desirable. Light from the rear, falling on the puppet's hair, produces a halo effect that makes the puppet stand out from the background.

The side lights are not essential, but, for variety, you could illuminate an entire scene with blue light coming from just one side. This would suggest moonlight, or a street light, creating a mysterious atmosphere because half the puppet is lit while the other side is dark. Another spooky effect can be created by lighting the puppet from below with a flashlight.

The scrim lights are aimed up at an angle to illuminate the scrim. Care should be taken to avoid hot spots, since the scrim looks best when lit as evenly as possible. Even though the scrim is at an angle, it will appear perpendicular to the audience which will see it as a solid wall of illuminated fabric.

Colored Lights

There are two ways to color the light falling on your stage: 1) Use gels (colored acetate) in front of ordinary white bulbs; 2) use colored light bulbs. Either way you are filtering the light. A red gel, for example, lets only red light pass and reflects back the other colors in white light. A red bulb, also, lets only the red light wavelengths pass. Therefore, colored lights are not as bright as white lights. Not all the light is passing through. It is important to take this into account when planning your lighting design.

If you use gels to color the light, be careful that they don't overheat and melt, warp, or catch fire. Buy acetate gels intended for such use and test the manner in which you plan to mount the gel by using it during your rehearsals.

Gels used in the professional theatre can withstand extreme heat. These you can tape right to the surface of a 100-watt bulb. Other acetate gels should be suspended a few inches away from the bulb. A coffee can or a reflector lamp shade works well as a frame to hold the gel.

When planning the colors to use, keep these psychological factors in mind: blue light recedes and red light advances. That is, the objects on stage will appear more distant and cooler under blue light; under red light, they will appear closer and warmer. Any white object on stage will appear the color of the bulb you use. However, other colors will be changed, sometimes with undesirable results, by a colored light source. For example, green scenery will look very dark, almost black, under red light. Be sure to try out your color combinations and make your aesthetic decisions early in the planning of your production.

Controlling Lights

A simple light control box can be constructed with materials available in any hardware store. If your stage will be using professional, high wattage, spotlights, you will need a large, high wattage, dimmer. The description included here is for the average person with modest resources.

A dimmer is a volume switch for light. Many kinds are available on the market today, designed to replace any switch in your house. They all warn that they are designed for permanent installation for the control of incandescent lights, and not for electric motors. Still, I have never had any problem using this kind of dimmer, "permanently" mounted in a portable light control box.

The top surface of the control box has only a few switches and the dials for the dimmers (3-5). The maze of wires, safely concealed inside, lead outlets along the back side of the box. The switches, dials, and outlets should be clearly labeled.

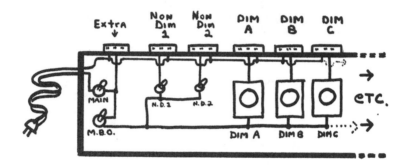

A. Front (key) lights.

B. Main (teaser) lights.

C. Foot lights.

3-5.   *A light control box.*

Following the circuit diagrammed in 3-5, from the plug on the left which brings in the power to your whole system, the first element is the master on/off switch (main). Ordinarily this is not used, but in an emergency you can easily shut everything off with it. The next element is the master black out switch (M.B.O.), which is used to turn off (or on) all the stage lights together. For convenience, an extra outlet is wired just before the M.B.O. This can be used to power your sound system, or for a small light illuminating the control box—things you would not want shut off with the lights during the show.

Wired to the M.B.O. are the controls for the stage lights: non-dim switches and dimmers. The non-dim switches are for illuminated scenery, or for any stage device requiring only on/off power. The exact number of dimmers on your control box depends on the number of lights in your stage. A typical application might find the scrim lights on one dimmer, the back and main lights on another, and the front and/or foot lights on the third dimmer. For flexibility, I suggest installing one more dimmer than you actually need. As your stage and needs grow, the extra dimmer may come in handy.

Along the back of the box are the outlets into which you plug your stage lights. Outlets with three sets of holes are best, so you can plug three banks of lights into one dimmer. Be sure to note the maximum wattage (usually 600W) for the dimmers you install and do not overload them.

Along the top of the diagram is a line leading back to the main power cord. This represents the wire that completes the circuit for all the outlets. The little U shapes in the line indicate that it does not touch the vertical lines bringing power to the outlets.

If this diagram does not make any sense to you, and you do not have any experience with electrical wiring, try to find someone who does to answer your questions, assist you, or even do the work for you. The other important construction notes are: 1) the main power cord should be heavy duty; 2) use solder on all connections of wire-to-wire; 3) use electrical tape to insulate any bare wires. I have found it handy to put the panel with the switches on a hinge, so the wires are accessible.

With a control box like this, you can fade the lights on or off in a variety of series. For example: first your scrim lights come on revealing your scenery in silhouette only. Next, your main lights come on. Finally, you bring up the front lights and your stage is fully lit.

You can keep the control box backstage where the puppeteers or a technician (light, sound, and prop person) can use it. However, if you have a large enough puppet group and can spare a person, the lights can be controlled from out front. It takes a lot of wire to reach the box, but the technician will be able to see the lighting effects from the audience's point of view. If you decide to use such a system, you might also want that person to control the sound from out front.

Special Effects

When appropriate, you might want to use any of the following special effects: strobe lights, black light, Christmas tree lights, snow light (mirrored ball), or fireplace (fake fire) light. In general, professionals look down on the use of gimmick devices. I don't categorically object to their use, unless they're used thoughtlessly. Most people have seen such effects many times before; strobe lights are no longer a novelty. You run the risk of having people think "Big deal," or "We've seen this before."

Ask yourself why you want to use such effects before you work them into your show. If the effect will really add something to the show, in terms of variety, visual impact, atmosphere or mood—use it. If you're just using it because you've got the equipment laying around—let it lay around.

These are the basics of stage lighting. It's up to you to experiment on your own and observe the methods of others. Use your imagination to discover simple ways to achieve variety. Even though the chief function of lights is to make the puppets visible to the audience, they can do more than go on at the beginning and off at the end.

Sound

When I refer to sound I include three separate things: music, sound effects, and voices. If you or other members of your puppet group are talented musicians, take full advantage of this resource by including live music in your show. Many interesting sound effects can also be created live.

Live voices are those portions of the dialogue and narration that are not prerecorded. Live voices may be amplified, but since high quality reproduction takes sophisticated equipment and know-how, it's often better to go the unamplified route. Your primary concern is that the audience be able to hear your show clearly. Lound sound distorted by cheap sound equipment will be no better than sound that is inaudible because of low volume.

Any performer will agree that it's important for the audience to hear the show, but there are two schools of thought concerning the methods appropriate for puppetry. Those who feel puppets should stick close to their roots as a folk art are likely to frown upon super-slick, show-business amplification techniques. On the other hand, puppeteers very conscious of their competition in the world of entertainment want their productions to compare favorably and conform with modern technical standards of excellence. The approach is up to you.

Live Unamplified Sound

A production with live unamplified sound will put a greater demand on the puppeteers in terms of diction and projection. The puppeteers will need to be coached, and they will have to practice especially hard. Live sound is not the easy way out. Indeed, this seemigly simpler approach can be harder on the performers than relying on microphones.

It is not necessary to amplify the sound of your puppet show if it is a small-scale production performed in intimate surroundings. The decision to use amplified sound depends on the location of your show and the ability of your puppeteers to project their voices. The Bread and Puppet Theatre of Vermont often performs outdoors, where electricity is unavailable. All their sound is live. A narrator in front of the stage uses a paper cone megaphone. This simple answer to the problem, used by the ancient Greeks is certainly effective. Greek theatre productions were held outdoors, in huge amphitheatres. The actors wore large masks with built-in megaphones to carry their voices over the entire arena. The effect is similiar to a cheerleader's use of a megaphone to reach the crowds in the stands.

Indoors, if you have a loud and strong voice you shouldn't require a megaphone. The walls of the hall will contain your voice enough to fill a fairly large room. However, once you start to perform in larger halls (gymnasiums, cafeterias, auditoriums), you should consider the use of amplified sound.

If you do not have sound equipment, and the puppets in your

production are to be manipulated by young children, I strongly advise an adult narrator in front of the stage. Not only does this solve the weak voice problem, but the children will not have to memorize the lines of dialogue. The narrator can tell the story and do the speeches of the puppet characters. The kids will have a great time providing the action. Children who watch the show will consider it quite entertaining to know that the puppeteers are other children.

I have mixed feelings about creating sound effects in front of the stage. Kids really seem to enjoy watching someone make the various noises required, but this side show can be quite distracting, drawing attention from the puppets. However, considering the short attention span of children and the need for the production to have variety in order to hold their interest, I sometimes like this approach. Once again, it's up to your personal tastes.

If you are using all three types of sound (music, sound effects, and voices) be sure that they are equally loud, and that no one element overpowers the rest. You may decide to combine unamplified and amplified sound in your show. If you do, take care to blend these elements harmoniously. They should complement each other, not compete.

Public Address Systems

Public Address (P.A.) systems consist basically of an amplifier, speakers, and a microphone. They are sometimes portable, and sometimes built into the theatre. If you're going to perform in a new location, try to find out as much as you can about the sound system. If possible, it is always best to inspect the site personally, preferably *before* the day you start unloading and setting up your show. If you can't look at it, be sure to get the following information about the P.A. system.

1. If they are planning to provide a P.A. system (usually specified in the contract), ask if there will also be someone provided to help set it up and operate it.
2. Is the system in regular use and in good working order, or has it been collecting dust for years in the basement?
3. Does the amplifier have provisions to accept external sound sources (your tape recorder and mike mixer)?
4. What kind of connecting patch cords will be required? Will you have to provide them yourself? Do they have the kind you need?
5. Can the level of sound be controlled conveniently backstage by you, or is it built into a closet off in the wings?
6. What kind of microphones are available? Lavaliere (neck) mikes don't require stands; any other type will.
7. Are the speakers built into the auditorium, or can they be set up close to your stage?
8. Will there be mike cords, speaker cords, and power extension cords provided?

Two things are most likely to go wrong with a P.A. system: an annoying hum coming through the speakers, and feedback. The hum is usually caused by equipment that is not properly grounded. If a tape recorder is used in conjunction with an amplifier, they must be mutually grounded. All the connecting patch cords must be in good shape and "in phase" (properly grounded), or you will get a hum.

Feedback is that horrible squealing that occurs as a result of poor use of speakers and microphones. When the sound coming from the speakers is picked up by a microphone, it is sent back out through the speakers again. This loop causes those horrible squeals. *The speakers cannot be placed in back of the microphones.* The speakers should be in front of your stage, aimed at the audience. Be sure the mikes themselves are aimed so that they do not pick up the speaker sound. Of course, there is a limit to the amplification level you can use before the volume reaches the microphones no matter which way they are aimed. Thus, it is important to have the volume controls hands. If they won't be right backstage with you, be sure someone is stationed at the controls during the entire show to ride the levels. A modern system will have VU meters to help the person controlling the sound level.

I hope you're lucky enough to have new equipment to work with. Such incredible advances have been made in the technology of sound reproduction that the fidelity (trueness to life) possible is ideal.

Tape Recorders

It is possible to prerecord the entire sound track of your production. It is also possible to combine live sound with prerecorded sound. For example: your music and sound effects could be on tape, while the dialogue is performed live. If you do combine sources, remember to pay particular attention to the volume levels. As I said before, the sources shouldn't compete with each other; they should blend together tastefully.

Effects and songs on tape should be separated with segments of leader tape. This is done by physically cutting the magnetic tape and splicing in the leader where required. With your sound tape arranged like this, it is possible to "cue-up" each effect.

Effect number one has just ended. The recorder is left running until the leader tape appears. Then it is stopped, and the tape is advanced by hand until the end of the leader (beginning of effect #2) is at the playback head. With the effect cued up like this, it will start immediately when needed. Recorders with instant stop buttons are the best to use for this type of operation. It is also important that the exact beginning of the effect be spliced to the end of the leader tape. There should be no silent space, or else there will be a slight delay when the instant stop button is released, before the effect starts. Since it is hard to edit on cassettes, I recommend reel-to-reel recorders only.

The best quality tapes are made by professional sound studios. Most large touring puppet productions use professional tapes. Trying to make your own professional tapes may disappoint you unless you have sophisticated equipment and technical expertise.

If your budget will not allow the purchase of a professional tape, you can make a usable tape yourself. Either a radio station or a rock band is likely to have the technical knowledge and the necessary equipment. Find a friend involved with either. If you have some modest equipment of your own, but not enough to do the job, rent the extra equipment: microphones and a mike mixer for example. Take the quietest room in your house, hand blankets on every possible surface, and you have a makeshift recording studio. Try to locate the recorder itself in the next room, so that the mikes don't pick up motor noises. With such a setup you can record your own music, singing, sound effects, and dialogue. Be sure to use the fastest tape speed: 7½ ips (inches per second) is the top on most recorders, but 15 ips yields essentially perfect results if you can get the equipment.

Use the best low-noise polyester magnetic recording tape available. It costs more than most other tapes, but is intended for professional applications. As a safety precaution, have a copy made of each tape sound in case the first one gets damaged or lost.

You can use either a tape deck to play back tapes or a tape recorder. A tape deck requires an external amplifier (such as a home stereo or P.A. system). A tape recorder has a built-in amplifier, and often built-in speakers too. However, since small speakers can't be played loudly without distorting the sound, don't rely on them. Instead, try to bypass the speakers and, if possible, the built-in amplifier. If you use only the P.A. system amp and speakers, you'll get much better results.

Remember: many pieces of music and most records are protected by copyright. This means if you use this material in a show and charge an admission fee, you need permission for use and you may have to pay a royalty fee. I know some puppeteers who freely rip off anything they want. I have been told by a professional puppeteer to use what I want until I get caught, and then play dumb. Apparently he felt that the chances of getting caught were slim. Frankly, I was shocked, considering how wide his exposure is. Personally I feel artists should respect other artist's property: If you can't pay the fee, create your own material, or use material that is in the public domain. I certainly do not advocate the illegal use of copyrighted material.

Prerecorded Dialogue

The advantage of having all the sound prerecorded, including the dialogue, is that you can do some very nice effects on the tape. Little musical bridges can fade in and out between the scenes; an abundance of sound effects can be included; background music can play during the entire show. It takes a supreme effort initially, but once you have the perfect tape you can use it as long as you like.

The disadvantage of prerecorded dialogue is that you can't play off audience reaction, and if anything goes wrong you can't ad-lib.

If you expect that the puppeteers in your show will have a hard time memorizing their lines or doing the voices, the prerecorded show will be ideal. You can even have professional actors read the lines, which tends to give very impressive results.

Even if you've recorded the dialogue, it's a good idea to know every line in the show and say them along with the tape. The audience won't hear you, but you will be able to bring back some of the intimacy and spontaneity to your production. You really have to feel the part to project life into your puppet. Saying or mouthing the words helps you get into character.

Keep in mind that it is hard to achieve excellent lip-sync when using prerecorded dialogue and puppets with articulated mouths. No matter how well you know the tape, you'll usually be half a beat behind the dialogue. This is especially noticeable at the end of a pause, when the speaking resumes but the puppeteer can't time the start exactly.

Sound Effects

Sound effects for puppet shows are really fun to create. Have you noticed the abundance and variety of noises Warner Brothers uses in their animated films? They really add a lot to the show. You can use them also. Whether you record them in advance or do them live, there are four main categories of sounds to consider: percussion, wind, string and mechanical.

Percussion effects include all types of crashes, and any two things hit together: pots, pans, garbage can lids, chains, drums, cymballs, chimes, bells, glass bottles, piano strings, and sheet metal, to name a few.

String Effects are made by any string musical instrument. You don't have to be able to play it—just get a noise out of it.

Wind Effects include Kazoos, bike horns, whistles, bugles, slide whistles, tubas, party favors, flutes, recorders, jaw harps, and tea kettles.

Mechanical Effects include electrical noises such as car horns, buzzers, doorbells, motors, sirens, cord organs, and electronically synthesized noises; mechanical sounds that are not electric, like egg beaters, saws, ratchets and music boxes.

Certain noises are obnoxious and others can be charming. Try to match the appropriate sound to your needs and stiuation. Remember that timing is very important when dealing with sound effects. Whoever operates the tape or makes the noise has to practice at your rehearsals to be right on cue.

Since certain sounds are hard to create and/or record, don't forget the tape will keep going regardless of the jam you may be in on stage. Furthermore, there is an intimacy that is lost in performing to a prerecorded voice track. As a puppeteer, it's no fun. I found being a manipulator only, not doing the voices, too mechanical an experience. However, some people are more comfortable doing performances this way. I suggest you try both ways to see which you like best.

about sound effect records. Electra Records has a marvelous catagogue of effects: rain, wind, explosions, automobiles, city noises, telephone noises and crowd noises as well as many others, are available. A nice assortment of creaks, moans, laughs, and other weird sounds can be taken from Halloween Party records. Make sure that the record is in good condition. Any scratches or surface noise will make the audience painfully aware that the sound came from a record. It is best to transfer the sounds you want to tape, and put them in the proper order, with leader tape between each effect, because it is hard to cue up recrds.

Although an abundance of effects is good, don't expect such effects to make a fantastic show out of a weak script that is poorly manipulated. Effects are icing on the cake. If the cake's rotten, all the pretty frills won't mean a thing.

And please remember to keep the effects subtle, and not to overuse any one effect. Unless the noise is part of a running gag throughout the production, once is usually enough. The last thing you want your audience to be saying, is "Alright already."

Music

Music is an essential element in any puppet production. No matter how small or large the show, careful thought should be given to choosing appropriate music. Your personal tastes will probably determine what you choose, but you must also consider your audience. You may have valid reasons for liking a particular song and wanting to turn the world on to it, but if it isn't appropriate for the show don't use it.

What makes a song appropriate varies with the situation, but certain generalizations can be made. The music used should not dwarf your production. For example, concert orchestra would more than dwarf a hand puppet show. Something quiet—acoustic guitars, flutes, or recorders—would be much better for a small-scale hand puppet show.

Certain instruments have a distinctive sound quality, called "sonority." These qualities can be especially effective when a particular tune and instrument is used to identify a particular character in your show. The best example of this identification if found in Prokofiev's "Peter and the Wolf." Each time a character appears, we hear the familiar instrument sound and melody.

The tempo of the music must also fit the occasion. Fast, lively music would be out of place in a sad scene and slow, melancholy music would obviously be inappropriate for a cheerful scene.

If you have talented musicians in your puppet group, try to take full advantage of them. Of course, you may find yourself having to politely persuade someone not to make his musical debut during your show after six weeks of guitar lessons. Such situations are never easy to handle, but if you're the director you're the boss and have the final decision. The members of your company must be prepared to go

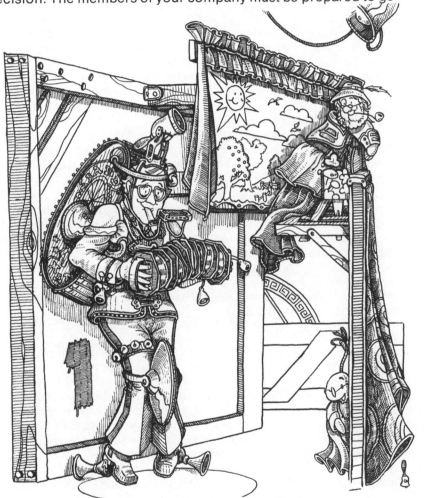

along with any aesthetic decision you make. Perhaps one of your members knows more about music than you do. This person should become the musical director. Give him authority and freedom to make decisions, but try to work closely together to achieve a unified production. The director of the production must retain the final authority, should there be a disagreement. Committee work is never easy, especially when you're dealing with creative people who have their own ideas about how things should be done. Hopefully, your group will see a unified production as the most important goal, and will subordinate their individual feelings for the achievement of the whole.

The person responsible for the musical direction has several options. The music may be prerecorded or live (as explained in the preceding section); it may be written especially for the show, adapted especially for the show, or taken straight as it is found in a written or recorded form.

Most contemporary arrangements and compositions are protected by copyright laws. However, a wide variety of older selections are in the public Domain. A copyright lasts forty years and is renewable once. After that, the music may be used without the necessity of a royalty fee. Someone can copyright a new *arrangement* of a piece in the public domain, however, so be sure to check if you plan to use music straight off a record.

If you want to (and are able to) write your own music, be sure that you also have singers and musicians to perform what you have created. Live or recorded, it will take talented people to produce the music for your show. For the most part, if members of your puppet group sing or play instruments, you won't have to worry about hassles with the musicians union. But if you need outside assistance, be prepared to pay the union scale—which is very high in comparison to what puppeteers earn for an evening's work. Having puppeteers who are also musicians will make a big difference in keeping your costs down. Even if you're not professional singers, everyone in your group (including the technicians) can and should join in the chorus. Remember that the audience doesn't expect the puppets to be the greatest singers in the world.

Music in Your Production

There are many ways in which music can become part of your production. Here are the most common ways to use music.

Music To Be Seated By. Before the show starts, put on a tape to set the mood. The selections you choose should have some relevance to the show—spooky music for a Halloween show, carols for a Christmas show, or electronic music for a space age adventure. If the show is basically an entertainment, perhaps circus music would establish a mood of frivolity. If the production is tongue-in-cheek "camp," ragtime music or 1930s jazz might establish a nostalgic tone.

Overture. Many productions include a musical opening, during which the house lights start to go dim—indicating to the audience that the show is beginning. The overture can be a special song or a medley of the songs that will be featured in the production. An overture is functional, because it gives people a chance to finish their conversations and become quiet before the curtain goes up.

Background Music. Instrumental music played very softly can provide a nice atmosphere for many scenes. Often the music is so quiet that the audience doesn't notice it, but they still are hearing it and responding to the mood. Underscoring with background music can help bring added suspense to a scene or establish an air of fun and comedy.

Show Tunes. Some songs are a part of the script. While they are being sung, the main focus of attention is on the music and lyrics. Most musicals are just a bunch of show tunes strung together by a flimsy plot. There are, on the other hand, serious dramatic productions that include a few show tunes for variety, comic relief, or to further the story development. Besides the central character (or characters), either a narrator (minstrel) or a chorus can sing the show tunes.

Musical Bridges. Between the end of one scene (or act) and beginning of the next, short musical passages can be used. These tie the scenes (or acts) together. Such musical bridges can also be used during a scene, if the characters are supposed to be traveling to a new location or waiting for time to pass.

Intermission Music. The same music used to seat the audience (or the overture) can be used during the intermission. Again, the audience should be given time to quiet down and get settled before the next act begins.

Finale. Unless the show is a serious and introspective drama, it should end with an intensely exciting finale. Musical finales are my favorite, because they are a sure way to wrap up the show in an entertaining fashion.

Music To Exit By. This is the time to sneak in your favorite rock and roll song, or anything else you want. If your finale has a very catchy tune, perhaps you should make the exit music an instrumental version of the finale. This will help make it stick in people's minds, and they will be humming it on their way home. Exit music should not start until the house lights are fully on and people have started to leave.

Musical Sound Effects. Another way to employ music in your production is to use various instruments to create sound effects. This can range from the kind of noise that anybody can get out of any instrument, to a precise melody expertly played.

Choosing Music for Your Production

One of the best ways to choose music for your production is to borrow records from the library. Of course, you can use records from your own collection, but I'm assuming that your record collection is fairly modest. If you have a broad knowledge of and familiarity with music you may not need to preview records from the library; otherwise, being able to sample a wide variety of records is extremely helpful.

Library records can be previewed either before or after you know just what you want. You may be looking for music that has an air of regal splendor (for the scene in the king's palace); serious and somber music (the hero is sent to the dungeon); suspenseful music (the hero makes his escape); joyful music (the hero is reunited with his lover).

Or, a certain piece of music may inspire a particular scene or even an entire production. The unique qualities of a composition may be ideal for a scene not in the production at hand. You may find yourself working it in, or saving it for the future. If you preview many records you will hear more than you can use in any one production. Try to take notes and catalogue what you hear.

Once you know what you want to use you will probably have to buy new records, because most library records have undesirable surface noise and skips. The new records can then be transfered to tape. This method is better than buying prerecorded tapes, because unless you can make a dub of the tape you'll have to cut and splice your original source to make the music fit the scenes.

Some puppeteers like to use music they feel is "puppety." They feel that only certain kinds of music are appropriate for puppet shows. This is a matter of personal taste. "Puppety" music is basically simple compositions that evoke a feeling of cuteness or fantasy—the kind of music that is found on most kiddie records. Although this is a perfectly valid approach, it is by no means essential. Just one day's viewing of *Sesame Street* will prove that children are no longer being marketed kiddie tunes. The songs used are as fully arranged and hip as any pop tune on the radio.

Whatever approach you take is fine, provided that you are pleased, your audience will be pleased, and your sponsor (if you have one) will be pleased as well. Marketing a production is not easy. Every person you ask is likely to give you a different opinion. I believe that you must first please yourself, and hope that the public will see things your way. Trying to figure out what your audience will like involves so much guess work that you might as well please yourself. You'll never be able to please everybody, so at least pick music you will be able to live with. If your show is any good, it's likely you'll be hearing that music quite a bit. By the end of the run you'll be pretty tired of hearing it anyway, so the last thing you should do is to start off with music you don't like.

Scripts

You should have a goal when you begin the task of writing a puppet show. The script created for a live puppet show is different from the one for film or videotape. Different, also, are the scripts written for a one-man show and a puppet company. It is really important to know in advance how the puppet show will be produced, because this will help you visualize the production as you write.

Puppetry is a unique form of theatre. As you work with puppets, and begin to understand their special abilities and limitations, you will be better equipped to create a script that is custom-made for puppets.

The more specifically you can define your audience and your purpose, the easier it will be to create a goal-oriented show. Some

(Page 1.)

Scene:

shows are purely entertainment; others mix in a little moral as a lesson; some mix a little entertainment into a script that is primarily designed to teach.

Know as much as possible about the size, age, location, and sophistication of your audience. A production conceived for adult audiences is different from one for child audiences. A show intended for audiences of all ages must be different from a specialized production. Remember that even though your script is in written form, the end result of your efforts will be acted in front of an audience.

Initial Planning

So many separate elements must be taken into account that there is no right or wrong place to start planning a puppet show. In general, one of the most helpful things is to organize your thoughts on paper. An inventory of your present situation will help you find a place to begin.

One of the first questions you should ask yourself is whether the story will be original or an adaptation of a fairy tale or poem. Even if you have decided to use a script you bought or found in a book, it's likely that you will be modifying it in some way. Sometimes I find that I have made so many changes that it would have been easier to start with the original source (poem or fairy tale) and adapt my own version.

Adaptation of a piece of literature relieves the scriptwriter of the responsibility of creating a substantially sound story. More effort can then be put into visualizing the production. The story is the foundation, and it must be strong. If you create a story that is dull and lacks human interest, suspense, or conflict, all the fancy production techniques will be icing on a rotten cake.

Another point in favor of adaptation is that most professional companies have found that wellknown tales draw more crowds than original stories. *Cinderella, The Emperor's New Clothes, The Three Little Pigs, Goldilocks, Little Red Riding Hood, Rapunzel, Snow White, Peter Pan, The Pied Piper, Puss in Boots, The Ugly Duckling, The Frog Prince, Gulliver's Travels* and *Jack and the Beanstalk* are but a few familiar stories you may want to produce. Perhaps the public feels more confident about attending a show with a story they already know. Bil Baird told me that he'd like to do more original stuff, but every season they have to include the tried and true moneymakers.

When reviewing stories and poems for possible adaptation, pay attention to the amount of action in the story. You want as much action as possible—but it should be limited to a few locations, and should be action that the puppets are capable of performing. Avoid complicated plots and wordy dialogue. You should interpret as much of the story as possible into things the puppets actually can *do*. The narrator or puppets can talk about things you can't *possibly* do on stage, but most of the story should be related directly through action the audience can witness.

Action scripts are harder to write than dialogue, but they are much more interesting to watch. If you were planning to do your puppet show over the radio, 95 percent of the available scripts would be fine. But if you want a visually stimulating show, be prepared for a lot of editing, rewriting, and hard work.

Developing a Puppet Script

Once you've decided on the story, its purpose, audience, and the type of puppets required, you're ready to start visualizing a puppet show. Visualizing is like running a movie in your mind's eye. Try to imagine what the audience will eventually be seeing. What does the set look like? How is it lit? How do the puppets look? What are they doing? Little by little, as you work out the answers to these questions and write down your ideas, you'll be developing a rough scenario of the plot and stage directions.

At this point, feedback from other people can be extremely helpful. Before you go on, evaluate and revise the fundamental elements of the production you're planning. Have you imagined elaborate staging beyond your means? Does your group have the time, money, and talent to carry out your grand plans? If not, cut back on the extras—but by all means save the brilliantly simple, intrinsically "puppet," ideas.

After this evaluation, rewrite and then type up the scenario. Distribute it to your puppeteers and run through it informally. You need not have the actual puppets that will be used, but it is helpful to put some sort of puppets on. The puppeteers will begin to find the characters into which you have cast them. Encourage them to experiment with several different voices, until they find one with which they are most comfortable. If there are obvious flaws in your casting, now is the time to try different arrangements. The object of these runthroughs is to learn how the puppeteers have interpreted the personalities of their assigned characters. You will also discover the ways in which the characters interact. The more improvising, interacting, and just plain horsing around you do the better. It's a good idea to leave a cassette recorder running during these runthroughs to catch lines improvised spontaneously that otherwise would be lost. The director and/or playwright should also take notes on choreography and pantomime situations that are invented during these sessions. The beauty of developing a puppet script this way is that it will be custom-made for the abilities and personalities of your puppeteers.

After a few of these sessions (at least two, on two separate occasions), go back to the typewriter to prepare a neat first draft of the script. The script should not be considered final at this point. Although it probably closely resembles the version that will be presented to the public, you should remain flexible and open to criticism and new ideas up until your dress rehearsals. After that, I feel it's best to close out changes and go with what you've got.

I should point out here that most Broadway musicals undergo drastic revisions on the road for up to a year before they open in New York. The cast often has to learn completely new songs and dance routines. This audience testing is intended to produce a hit—show with mass popularity. You too may want to revise your show during your season or tour, but I believe that if you really work hard during your rehearsals you can determine your final script before you begin your dress rehearsals.

The advantage of making no drastic changes after dress rehearsals begin is that you can then use this time to tighten up the show. Until the puppeteers (and technicians, if there are any) understand that no further changes will be made, they cannot really concentrate on efficiency of motion on and off stage. It just doesn't make any sense to figure out a way to conduct the swiftest possible scene change if there's a chance the scene will be cut. On the other hand, it's reasonable to ask that the tempo of the entire show be made livelier once everyone knows that this is the final version.

Usually, the director is the person responsible for the selection or creation of the script. The development of the script can be a group effort, but don't try to produce a show with more than one director. To achieve a unified production requires the vision of one person: the director.

As a coach and leader, the director must be sensitive to the feelings of the people in the production. The director is boss, but the puppeteers are not slaves. In fact, the director functions as servant to the puppeteers, coaching their performance from the point of view of the audience. Hopefully, the people with whom you work will respect each other, and the function and contribution of each.

The Structure of a Puppet Script

There are several ways to organize your script on paper. No matter which you choose, you must structure your story around the three basic dramatic elements: the beginning, the middle, and the end.

The Beginning. The first scene of your production should establish the time and place of your story. The characters should be introduced to the audience and their relationship to each other and the story should be made clear. Assume the audience has never heard your story before, even if you are adapting a well-known fairy tale.

Once you have established the situation, you should start to develop the conflict of the story. The problem can be introduced immediately or foreshadowed. By foreshadowing, or hinting at the troubles yet to come, you increase the intrigue and suspense of the story. Try to get the audience to worry along with your characters. It's very important that the audience care what happens next if you are to hold their interest.

The Middle. Your story should reach a climax during the middle of your play. Your goal in developing the crisis is to involve the audience with the puppets' predicament. Make the audience share the fear of your characters—their emotional involvement guarantees that their interest will be sustained.

As the suspense of your story builds, be sure to have some comic relief periodically. It is impossible to keep the suspense at a high pitch. Instead, approach the climax through ever-increasing tension interupted with periods of relaxation.

The End. The problem of the story is resolved at the end. This denouement does not have to be in favor of the hero. In a tragedy, the hero does not overcome his or her obstacle, but rather is beaten by the villian or by fate. In a comedy, the antagonist (villian) is beaten by the protagonist (hero) and the ending is happy. Comedy and tragedy in this classic sense do not refer to funny or sad, but to the eventual resolution of the conflict with which the play deals.

Examples of Script Structure

The following examples of puppet scripts are provided as models for you to follow. They are all standard formats. No one format is better than any other, so choose the type you like best. Your final version can be double-spaced but your rough draft should be triple-spaced to allow room for editing notes and revision.

#1 Dialogue Format.

Narrator

Once upon a time, though it wasn't in my time, and it wasn't in your time, and it wasn't in anybody else's time, there was a . . .

Jester
(pops up)

Now wait just a minute. If it wasn't in your time, or my time, or anybody else's time, that would be no time at all.

Narrator

That's right, that's fairy tale time.

Jester

Phoowee!

(exits down)

#2 Dialogue Format.

MM: (pats the piper on his back) Piper, you're forgetting what's happened.

PP: Yes, I forgot, and I thank you a lot. But I haven't forgotten that Falsestaff is rotten and there's sweat on my brow to think where he is now. (he shivers and cowers in the corner)

MM: (walks towards him) Oh, don't worry yourself over him my boy. Falsestaff is nowhere in sight.

FS: (spotlight from below lights the face of Falsestaff, who appears above the stage. He whispers to the audience.) Don't be so sure. Falsestaff has one more trick up his sleeve before he's ready to give in. (exit) (insane laughter is heard offstage)

PP: It's funny, but I almost feel the evil presence of that heel.

#3 Dialogue Format.

1. Old Woman: (sweeping up the inside of her cottage) Dear me, this house is such a mess. I'm really not ready for this play to begin.
2. Sound: Knock, Knock, Knock.
3. Old Woman: But there, I hear some knocking at the door already. (she sets the broom in the corner, fixes up her hair in the mirror.)
4. Sound: (louder) Knock, Knock, Knock.
5. Old Woman: Alright, I'm coming. (the broom falls over as she goes to the door and it hits her in the face, sending talcum powder dust all over.) (screams) AHHHHH!!! Oh no, Drat, oh now what shall I do, oh fie, fie?

#4 Pantomime Script Format.

Music fades, stage lights up. B1 comes in with his bag of candy. Sees the house and double takes. Sets down the bag. Puts his mask on; is about to ring the doorbell when he hears a weird noise. Looks around and sees nothing. When his back is turned, his bag of candy is replaced by a box. He double takes when he sees it. Cautiously he approaches it, looks all around it, laughs nervously, timidly touches it. The lid bursts open and ghosts fly out. B1 backs away and shivers. A worm puppet comes out of the box, walks around, and then goes back in the box. B1 approaches the box, looks inside, sees nothing; he scratches his head. Calls for the little worm: "Hey little worm, come back!" Huge monster worm appears. Lights flash on and off. Blackout. Spotlight immediately fades up, center stage, on the original bag of candy, in the place where it and the box had been.

Chapter 4

Perfecting Your Technique

A professional puppeteer must be disciplined mentally and physically. You must build up the strength and coordination of certain muscles in your arm, at the same time gaining fluidity and sensitivity to the movements of your fingers, wrist, arm, and body. Your entire self must be involved with the puppet even though the audience may not see the movements of your body. Remember that you are trying to project emotions to the audience through the puppet. Just as a stage actor must get "into character," you must really feel the joy or sorrow your puppet is supposed to be feeling. Your face may not be seen, but your voice will carry its expression—if you're really into your character. Don't be embarrassed about making funny undignified faces like those you made when you were a kid. The wall that hides you from the audience should be the great lifter of inhibitions. No one (except possibly your fellow puppeteers) will see that silly face, so try to be as loose as possible. Your puppeteering will be much better for the effort.

Practice Exercises

Persons trained in acting for the legitimate theatre have a head start. Concentration is a skill that must be practiced, and actors do many excercises to discipline their minds and bodies. Such experience is handy for a novice puppeteer. If you are interested in developing your ability to concentrate, you first must be totally serious about the practice. It is hard work, not a game. Although you may not be able to see immediate benefits to your labor, you will receive your gratification later, when your puppeteering starts improving.

A good exercise for concentration and coordination is the birth-life-death pantomime routine. The actor starts out on hands and knees with his head tucked down, resembling a rock. No movement at all occurs for a while. Then, slowly, this embryo comes to life. The actor's imagination and involvement with the different stages of human existence may find him discovering his hands, crawling, walking, eventually getting old, dying.

What makes this exercise so difficult is that the movements must be done slowly but smoothly. Try the excercise. You will see the degree of concentration needed to keep your mind on what you're doing, ignoring external stimuli. The concentration and the coordination you develop through this exercise in focusing will improve your puppeteering.

Movement Exercises

The following practice exercises are intended for a solo puppeteer using hand puppets. Although they were designed to be pantomime routines, you may find an occasional groan or gasp necessary. Do not, however, say any words or rely too heavily on sounds to get the meaning across to your audience. After experimenting and practicing with the routines, you should test them out on a few friends. If they don't understand what you're supposed to be doing, find out where they are becoming confused and rework your acting. Remember that the first few seconds of your routine are very important. If the audience is misled in the beginning, it may be impossible to get them back on track. They will start interpreting your actions to fit the wrong premise with which they began. Consider that your routine begins the second you make your entrance. Do not make any motions that are unnecessary or inconsistent with the skit.

#1. Enter as if you are climbing stairs at a moderate rate. When you reach the stage, look all around the surface of the playboard as if you have dropped something and are searching for it. You can't find it, so you look up, see the audience for the first time, and double take. Look quickly to the left and then to the right. You've discovered you're all alone on stage, so you cover your eyes and disappear from sight (straight down).

#2. Enter as if it is a big struggle to reach the playboard. Pretend something is pulling you down (lead shoes, quicksand, a monster, something sticky). You strain to get free. Finally, on your biggest tug, you become unstuck go flying across the stage, landing on your face. Remain there a moment. Then breathe heavily, as if you're trying to catch your breath. Finally, rise to an upright position. Give a sigh of relief—and instantly you're pulled under.

#3. Enter with your head bent way down and your hands fidgety (roll them). Pace back and forth the full stage a few times without looking up. Finally, stop in the middle of the stage and slowly turn your head to the audience. Look out into the audience, using a hand to suggest you're looking way out into the horizon. Lean out as far as you can. Lose your balance and fall down, using your hands to break the fall. Rise stiffly to your feet, rubbing sore spots. Begin pacing again, glancing out to the audience occasionally. Eventually, start to leave. Give one final look; shake your head in disgust; slowly turn and exit. Come back to take another peek at the audience from the spot you just left. Improvise a series of exits, peeking out at the audience from many different locations on stage.

#4. Enter as if you're carrying a small object. Set it down on the playboard. Pretend you're yelling to someone in the distance; wave to them. Then pick up the imaginary object (a softball), and throw it to your friend. Watch the flight of the ball. Clap when your friend supposedly catches it and signal for it to be thrown back. Watch it approaching and catch it. Do the same sequence of actions once more. Throw it for the third time, but when it comes back to you it's thrown high. Jump for it, but miss. Look around for it, scratch your head, then yell to your friend and shake your head (no). Look around some more, then see it. Clap your hands and jump for joy. Yell to your friend; point to the ball and nod your head (yes). Pick up the ball, wave goodbye to your friend, and exit.

#5. Slip onto the stage quietly. Be discovered lying down on your side, with your back to the audience. Pretend you're sleeping and breathing slowly (arch the body up and down, pivoting slightly on the head). Suddenly jerk your head up and look at the audience. Rise slowly rubbing your eyes; yawn and stretch. Do some jumping jacks. Touch your toes and do some push-ups. Move to a new spot and pretend your washing your face, shaving, brushing your teeth, etc. When you're all ready to leave, lie down and go back to sleep. Roll off the stage to exit.

#6 Enter like a sneak. Your head pops up for a second, looks suspiciously in all directions, and then appears somewhere else to make sure the coast is clear. Tiptoe quietly in. Check out all directions, nervously. When you get to center stage, start to tap the playboard in a few spots. When you've found the right spot, check in all directions first, then start digging a hole. As you dig deeper, your puppet should sink until just the head is visible. Climb out of the hole, check in all directions, then exit to get your treasure. Enter carrying an invisible but very heavy object. Put it in the hole and cover it up. Stop occasionally to make sure no one is watching. When the object is covered, pat down the dirt and exit.

#7. Enter crawling. The hands pull the puppet across the playboard. When you get to the other side, try to stand up—but you're drunk, and have a hard time keeping your balance. Your motions should resemble a waltz: one-two-three, one-two-three, each time catching your balance in a different direction. Keep it subtle but convincing. Eventually you get tired of trying to stand up, so you lie down. You can't get comfortable, so you rise again, holding your hands to your aching head. Knock your head against the playboard a few times to try to beat the hangover. Finally, put your hands to your stomach as if you're sick; quickly cover your mouth and exit.

#8. Enter ice skating. Your motions should be smooth, as if you're really gliding back and forth on the stage. When you slow down, you start to shake and then fall down. You try to rise, but can't. Crawl to the edge of the pond to stand up. After you're done rubbing sore spots, start to make a snowman. Roll up a large ball and place it center stage. Then roll a medium-size ball and put it on the first. Finally, roll the small one for the head and place it on top. Be sure not to walk through the imaginary spot where you've built the snowman. Walk around it. Step back to examine your masterpiece. Give it a few looks, then shake your head (no) and approach it. Remove the head, fuss with it, and put it back. Do this several times. Finally, smash the snowman to pieces and leave in disgust.

#9. Enter crying. Don't make any noise, but rub your eyes, rub your nose, and shake the puppet as if it is sobbing and breathing heavily. All of a sudden you see some flowers and stop crying. You go up to them, smell them, and start picking some. Place them in a bundle in one hand. When you have enough, smell the bunch with a long deep sniff. Exhale slowly to suggest your enjoyment of their scent, and exit skipping.

#10. Enter merrily. Gaze into the horizon. Become a fly fisherman, casting out his line into the distance. Reel the line in an cast out again. Do this several times until you get a bite. Struggle with this catch, reeling in and pulling on the imaginary pole. Finally your line goes slack, you lose your balance, and you fall down. Rub your eyes and slowly reel in the line with your head bent down. Sigh, and exit sadly.

Each of these ten pantomime routines requires you to be in complete control of your puppet. Your object is to have the audience understand what the puppet is thinking. Therefore, your control over where the puppet appears to be looking is extremely important.

Every puppet has a point where its eyes appear to focus. If yours doesn't, something should be done to correct the situation. Besides being so important in getting a pantomime routine across to an audience, eyes with a well-designed focus can really help to bring a character to life in the minds of your audience. They believe a puppet actually can see when good manipulation is applied to a puppet with a well-defined focus. Therefore, you must learn the difference between looking into the horizon and looking at the audience. Also practice watching objects in flight. Sometimes ignorance of the audience's presence is required, so practice movements on stage that clearly let the audience know that the puppet hasn't spotted them. Remember that every puppet has a slightly different point of focus, so you must devote time to master the control of each character that you own.

If you set up a mirror when you rehearse these routines, you will be able to see the actions from the vantage point of your audience. This will help you perfect the eye contact. You will also be able to easily spot when the puppet appears to sink. A full-length mirror (the kind designed to go on the back of a door) suspended horizontally is ideal. The mirror can be placed either above or below the playboard level (4-1). In either case it will be necessary to remove the front curtain of your stage so that you can see the mirror. If this is impossible, construct a mock-up of your stage playboard complete except for the front wall. I suggest a mock-up so that you get used to the actual height and width of your stage. However (and this is a big however) don't let the hassle of constructing a nice practice playboard keep you from practicing. Use your imagination. Set up anything as a wall: a ping pong table, an old door, a card table, miscellaneous scrap lumber, an old cardboard box. You can even use a tightly stretched rope, provided you have two sturdy points to which to tie it. Later on, when you've the time and money and motivation, you can build something a little more permanent. The main point is to get in there and do it. Just spend a little time on a regular basis as often as you can practicing and playing around with your puppets.

4-1.   How to set up a mirror for practice exercises with hand puppets.

Group Practice Sessions

Some of the best experiences I've had with puppetry have happened during informal group practice sessions. The mood is entirely different from a rehearsal. During a rehearsal, the puppeteers are perfection-oriented. The goal is to tighten up and polish a memorized show. Improvisations (improvs), on the other hand, are much looser, made up on the spot, and short. The ability to ad-lib is difficult at first, but with experience it becomes easier and more fun.

Most improvs are done with two puppets and two puppeteers. More than two may be used, but beginners should stick to pairs. When three or more puppeteers try to share the dialogue and contribute to the evolving story line, things can get confusing.

A typical improv is set up in this manner. Two characters and the situation in which they find themselves in are made up. (Opposite characters are ideal because conflict will be obvious in their relationship.) The puppeteers can either take a minute to decide on an ending, or they can start cold with no plans for where the plot will go. Advanced performers might start without even telling each other what type of character they plan to be. But unless you've done many improvs before you're better off deciding on characters, situation, and ending before you start.

The hardest thing, once you've begun your improv, is figuring out how to get off stage. Usually, the preplanned punch line does the trick. If you come to an obvious place to stop short of your punch line, take your exit. Don't stick rigidly to your planned exit line if you've stumbled on one just as good. Keep the improv under three minutes in length, and keep it full of lively, fast-paced action. No matter what happens, don't stop and whisper to the other puppeteer. Have the puppet communicate your intentions. If the improv isn't getting anywhere exciting, go off on a tangent. Be as crazy as you like, but keep it going!

The following thirty improv ideas are designed for two puppeteers and two puppets. Even though I've included a suggestion for a resolution, you might want to invent one of your own. If you're having a session with several puppeteers, try this: copy the improvs on slips of paper to be drawn out of a hat. Put the characters and situation on one side and the suggested resolution on the other. Then, when a pair is chosen, they draw a slip from the hat and read the characters and situation to themselves. If they can't think of an ending they can turn it over and use the suggestion. Even if they do invent an ending, they might want to turn it over to compare and choose the better of the two endings.

The success you have with these improv ideas will depend on the frame of mind of the puppeteers. The ones that seem funniest when you read them may bomb, and the corniest ones may turn out great. How well the puppeteers know each other and how uninhibited they are will make the difference. Just remember it's all for fun, so make a party out of it.

Improvisation Exercises:

#1. Characters: Dumb secretary and impatient boss.
Situation: Boss needs a letter typed in a hurry.
Resolution: He types it and she dictates it.

#2. Characters: Schoolteacher and disobedient student.
Situation: Student is a know-it-all in everything but his lesson.
Resolution: He stays after school to write Einstein's Special Theory of Relativity 100 times.

#3. Characters: Shopkeeper and thief.
Situation: The thief steals things when the shopkeeper isn't looking.

Resolution: When the thief leaves he discovers that the shopkeeper has picked the wallet from his pocket.

#4. Characters: Farmer and traveling salesman.
Situation: The farmer is more shrewd than the salesman.
Resolution: The farmer sell the farm to the salesman.

#5. Characters: Nurse and patient.
Situation: The patient is only pretending to be sick.
Resolution: The patient eats the food the nurse serves and really gets sick.

#6. Characters: Fireman and policeman.
Situation: They each envy the other's job.
Resolution: They both quit and become brain surgeons.

#7. Characters: Brother and sister.
Situation: Each has only a few cents.
Resolution: They pool their money and buy an ice cream cone to share.

#8. Characters: Music instructor and student.
Situation: Student can't sing.
Resolution: The student quits and becomes a rock 'n' roll star.

#9. Characters: Beggar and a rich man.
Situation: Rich man is asked to give spare change.
Resolution: The smallest bill the rich man has is a 100 dollar bill, so he tears it in half.

#10. Characters: Librarian and child.
Situation: Child can't find any book to read.
Resolution: Child should learn to read first.

#11. Characters: Banker and bank guard.
Situation: They're worried about recent chain of robberies.
Resolution: They decide to lock up the bank and stay home in bed.

#12. Characters: Artist and model.
Situation: Model keeps moving during the pose.
Resolution: He ties her up to sketch her.

#13. Characters: Detective and assistant.
Situation: No clues on their newest case.
Resolution: They make up clues to see where it gets them.

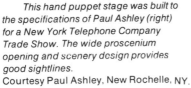

This hand puppet stage was built to the specifications of Paul Ashley (right) for a New York Telephone Company Trade Show. The wide proscenium opening and scenery design provides good sightlines.
Courtesy Paul Ashley, New Rochelle, NY.

For the brief cow-selling scene in Jack and the Beanstalk, a simple tree can suggest an entire forest. The backdrop itslef could be wider, though, for the people sitting on the extreme sides of the audience. Puppets by Donald Ave.
Courtesy Puppets with a Purpose, Spring Valley, Calif.

Experimental television puppets in a three-dimensional setting that combines excellent use of lighting and stylized scenery. Seen here are Desi the Bat and Gilbert the Frog, puppets made by Dan Peeler for Bill Stokes Associates of Dallas, Texas. Photo by Don Stokes, courtesy Dan Peeler

The scenery created by solo puppeteer Dick Myers is always in total harmony with the show. His designs have a pleasant, cartoon-like simplicity.
Courtesy Dick Myers, Hyde Park, NY.

Here's a perfect example of simplicity from the Poppinjay Puppet production of Three Little Pigs in Mexico. Puppeteers Roger Dennis and Bob Vesely have provided the audience with all the scenery that's required: a simple brick house.
Courtesy Poppinjay Puppets

Because few rod puppets are able to grasp and pick up props, the props also must be controlled from below by rods. This character, by Alan Stevens of The Smithsonian Puppet Theatre, is Queen Achren from The Book of Three. Photo by Mark Kinnaman, courtesy A. Stevens

The Magistrate from Bil Baird's Pinocchio.

The most important ingredient in a puppet company is enthusiastic puppeteers. Seen here are Susan Cassidy (top), Bob Youngman (center), and Joan Medford (bottom), who call themselves the Whistle Stop Puppeteers. Their theatre is a red caboose in Monterey, California.
Courtesy Richard Byrd

Pierrot, Columbine, and Harlequin in a scene from the Bil Baird's Marionettes production, Pinocchio. Photo by Nat Messik, courtesy of Frank Rowley

These puppet musicians (by the Riede Marionettes of Upland, Calif.) have been specially desgined to manipulate the props permanently attached to them.
Courtesy Richard J. Riede

Marionettes by Jerry Halliday of The Chrysler Museum Puppet Theatre, Norfolk, Virgina.

Courtesy Frank Dill

Mother Goose, designed by Phil Morrison of Northridge, California.
Courtesy Sidney Lee

Some productions are designed to be performed in the streets. The masked puppeteer/dancers of the Bread and Puppet Theatre were photographed during a peace march in Washington, D.C., in 1971.
Photo by Jim Crawford,
Courtesy of Mrs. Peter Schuman,
Plainfield, Vt.

Hand puppets can have props attached to them offstage. These characters by Martin Stevens do battle in an educational film called The Toymakers.
Courtesy Steven's Puppets,
Middlebury, Ind.

Bob Vesely and Roger Dennis have strong arms that won't sink. Like most professional puppeteers, they have developed the strength and coordination of their arms to the point that they don't have to think about them. Instead, they can concentrate on characterization.
Courtesy Poppinjay Puppets,
Cleveland, Ohio

Burr Tillstrom is seen here with his famous trio: Kukla, Fran, and Ollie. A pioneer in the field of televised puppetry, the Kuklapolitan players were performing daily on live television broadcasts over 25 years ago. The shows were usually improvised around rough skit ideas developed in weekly production planning sessions.
Courtesy Burr Tillstrom, Chicago, Ill.

#14. Characters: King and princess.
Situation: Life in the palace is dull.
Resolution: They call up Rent-A-Dragon so a knight can come to save them.

#15. Characters: Old witch and modern witch.
Situation: They disagree on the correct spells to use.
Resolution: The old witch sees things the new way and they both go off to a woman's liberation meeting.

#16. Characters: Tax collector and a prince.
Situation: Not enough tax money has been coming in.
Resolution: Tax collector borrows money from the prince, which he immediately turns in to save his neck.

#17. Characters: Soldier and cook.
Situation: The food tastes terrible.
Resolution: They feed it to the enemy as a new secret weapon.

#18. Characters: Barber and hippie.
Situation: Hippie won a free haircut but wants to trade in the prize.
Resolution: Barber gives him a bottle of flea shampoo instead.

#19. Characters: Athlete and poet.
Situation: Athlete doesn't like the poet's poems.
Resolution: Poet recites ball game scores like poetry.

#20. Characters: Baker and delivery boy.
Situation: Delivery boy keeps eating the goods on deliveries.
Resolution: He will deliver only frozen baked goods.

#21. Characters: Truck driver and waitress.
Situation: The coffee tastes like mud.
Resolution: Use something that wasn't "ground" yesterday.

#22. Characters: TV repairman and housewife.
Situation: TV only works when the set is upside down.
Resolution: Watch while standing on your head.

#23. Characters: Drunk and Salvation Army lady
Situation: Each wants to convert the other.
Resolution: They end up giving each other their spare change.

#24. Characters: School principal and superintendent.
Situation: Too many kids caught smoking in the bathrooms.
Resolution: Remove the cigarette machines from the bathroom.

#25. Characters: Two spirits.
Situation: People aren't afraid of ghosts these days.
Resolution: Become dentists; People are still scared of them.

#26. Characters: Shoe salesman and customer.
Situation: Lady has only $10 for $20 pair of shoes.
Resolution: Buy only one shoe.

#27. Characters: Mailman and postmaster.
Situation: Mail sent across town on Tuesday doesn't arrive until Saturday.
Resolution: Pick up the mail on Monday.

#28. Characters: Bartender and waitress.
Situation: The food is too cold and the drinks are warm.
Resolution: The bartender should serve the food and the waitress should make the drinks.

#29. Characters: Magician and his manager.
Situation: Manager wants a bigger percentage of the performance fee.
Resolution: The magician makes the manager disappear.

#30. Characters: Lion tamer and psychiatrist.
Situation: The lion tamer has lost his nerve.
Resolution: He should join a flea circus.

Developing Voices

The speech aspects of puppetry are perhaps the hardest to describe in writing. They cannot be diagrammed or photographed. The most important thing I can tell you is to listen to the speech patterns of others. Television is a source for a wide variety of voice characterizations. Movie stars, animated cartoons, even personalities in commercials all exhibit some form of "put-on" voice. Actors are often expected to speak in voices other than their natural, everyday voice. Some have only a small repetoire of characters; others, have an amazingly large number of voices they can do.

The acquisition of each new voice is a result of 1) careful listening, 2) mimicking, and 3) practicing. If you won't be disturbing anybody, try to mimic the voices you hear the next time you watch television. Repeat each phrase you hear. At the beginning, you probably will not sound too like the original, but try to listen more closely to the voice and to your impersonation of it. Ask yourself where the differences occur. Experiment with your voice by trying a variety of impersonations. You will be discovering the range of your voice. You may find certain voices impossible; others may be quite easy. Before long, you won't need to be mimicking voices just heard in order to sound correct. Part of your practice is trying to remember the particular qualities of each voice. Then the next time you hear the voice you can compare it with your memory for accuracy. This reinforcement of the remembered pattern should be continued until you get the voice down pat.

Don't underestimate the non-television sources that are available to you. The streets are full of characters. Shopkeepers, cab drivers, receptionists—practically anyone with whom you come into contact is a potential source for a new character. Naturally, the people that you run into more than once are better, so that you can check your impersonation against the actual character. The more you practice impersonating voices the easier it will be for you to analyze and zero in on the unique qualities that make a particular person's voice interesting. If you learn to listen and mimic, not only will you learn about the natural range of your own voice, but you'll increase its flexibility.

Once you've discovered your range, you can start to concentrate on a few voices. At first you should experiment with as many types as possible, so that you can discover just what your voice capability is. Do not try to develop a wide repetoire too fast, however, start with one or two voices. When you have those developed strongly, start to add more. A long list of character voices that are weak and only partially developed is less useful than taking the time to fully develop one character at a time.

In choosing voices to work on, try to pick ones that are not similiar to one another. Once you have discovered the range of your voice, you should be able to find total opposites for the first two voices you develop. Naturally, as you acquire more voices it gets harder and harder to keep the similarities to a minimum. Even so, you should be able to give new voices unique twists that make them distinctive.

Developing Characters

Voice quality is only one element of what makes a character interesting. The other part is the personality of that character. Developing charming and believable characters takes time. Voices can often be made up instantly, but to understand how a character would react to any given situation requires a familarity with that character which only time and practice can yield. Try to really live with each character. Substitute the voice you have invented for your real voice, and go about an otherwise normal day. It may sound crazy, but the more you speak in that character's voice the more you will develop it into an alter ego of your own personality. Hidden parts of your own personality will come to the surface through the various character voices you develop. This phenomenon makes puppetry a valuable psychotherapeutic tool. Some people have been able to express, through a puppet, feeling that could not otherwise be expressed despite countless therapy sessions. Puppets are able to do and say what people ordinarily cannot. Puppets have critized kings and propagandized the masses under the protective cloak of their innocent looks. The audience accepts a message that to which they would have closed their ears if the speaker had been human. Likewise, the puppeteer is able to say the unspeakable without his or her human inhibitions. This relationship between puppeteer and audience is vital for you to understand. If it's not crystal clear to you already, it will be after practical experience in the puppet world.

Since the puppet will free you from being responsible for your conduct, take advantage of this freedom artistically. Be as outrageous, or silly, or insane as you like when you're experimenting with new puppet voices and characters.

Review the following list of character types and imagine the voices possible for each. Then choose one and actually speak in that voice for a while, testing out the expressions appropriate for a variety of moods. You should also try to laugh, sneeze, cry, cough, and sing in a manner consistent with the character's personality.

A stupid screwball type—i.e., hillbilly or jester.
A stuck-up type—i.e., royalty or society lady.
A cute type—i.e.,an animal or child.
A wise guy type—i.e., bratty brother or punk hoodlum.
An elderly type—i.e., grandfather, grandmother, or witch.
A bird type.
A monster type (fierce or lovable).
A giant with a deep resounding voice.
A sly fox type—i.e., thief or detective.
A mad scientist type.
A jovial merchant type—the typical nice guy.

Keep in mind that puppetry is an action medium. A charming voice and dynamic personality needs to be accented with thoughtful and expressive movement. Don't rely too heavily on voice, or your character may be visually quite dull. However, do not try to keep the action at a peak constantly. Be subtle; save exaggerated motions for special occasions. The same is true for the volume of your speech. If you are always very loud and excited, you will have nothing new to do when you want to appear loud and excited.

Manipulation of Puppets With Mouths.

A puppet with a mouth can do more than open and close that mouth. With his wrist, a puppeteer can tilt the head from side to side and move it forward and back, up and down. The expressiveness of a mouthed puppet comes from combining these movements with the opening and closing of its mouth. For example: Astonishment mixed with disbelief can be expressed by jerking the head back and tilting it to one side as the lower jaw hangs open. Amazement can be as simple as leaning forward, eyes fixed on the remarkable object, while the head moves slightly from side to side as if gesturing "no."

For the most part, the mouth on a puppet is used to suggest that the puppet is actually speaking. The more you can make the mouth movements correspond to each syllable of speech the more convincing your puppet will be. I find it convenient to borrow a film term when discussing this kind of manipulation: the term "lip-sync" is used by film editors when they are trying to match the motion picture sound with the picture. Their goal is to get the speech of the actors synchronous with the movements of the actors' lips. Similarily, in puppeteering the puppeteer trys to match movement with sound.

A good way to practice lip-sync is to play a record with which you are very familiar. You probably know every pause and syllable of your favorite lyrics; therefore, if you play these songs and try to mouth the words with your puppet, it will feel almost as if you're doing the singing yourself. In fact, it's a good idea to sing along with the record as you practice using a puppet with a mouth. One of the goals of your practice is to develop the link between your brain and your hand muscles. Eventually it will become second nature for you to flawlessly sync the movements. You don't have to concentrate on making your tongue work properly; neither, in time, should you have to concentrate on your thumb movements.

In choosing the songs with which to practice, remember that instrumental passages should be short or, better still, nonexistent. At first, slow tunes will be easier. As you get better you can tackle faster lyrics.

When words have more than one syllable, you should open and close the mouth quickly at least twice. For instance, in counting to ten the mouth should open and close eleven times (the number seven requires two quick movements). Put on a puppet with a working mouth and have it count from ten to twenty. The open and close movements would be: ten: once; eleven: three times (quickly); twelve: once; thirteen: twice; fourteen: twice; fifteen: twice; sixteen: twice; seventeen: three times; eighteen: twice; nineteen: twice; and twenty: once or twice. The number of movements for multisyllable words often depend on the speed of speech. The word "twenty" is two distinct syllables when said slowly; however, if it is said quickly you might have time for only one movement.

One final pointer about good lip-sync manipulation: the words are supposed to look as if they are being formed in and coming out of the puppet's mouth. Try to make small forward movements for each syllable as the mouth opens. It's almost as if you are throwing the words out of the mouth. If you can keep this additional movement subtle, your lip-sync manipulation will become very sophisticated and professional.

The Ten Biggest Mistakes Beginning Puppeteers Make

Beginning puppeteers make many mistakes—and so for that matter—do experienced puppeteers. Expect to make mistakes as you learn. There is nothing wrong with making mistakes unless you have placed yourself so high up on a pedestal that you can't see (or won't admit) the mistakes you make. The goal of any artist should be continual self-improvement. I hope that I never have so large an ego that I close my mind to constructive criticism.

There are more than ten things puppeteers can do wrong. However, I have selected the ten mistakes I see most often in student productions: sinking, breaking character, weak voice projection, irregular characterization, poor eye contact, out of sync motion, wordy scripts, complicated plots, scene changes too long and too many, and poor finales. A list of the top twenty mistakes might add lack of directorship, too many props, voices too similar, bad lighting, unmotivated action, distractive stages and scenery, bad acting and showmanship, rip-off puppet creations, heavy use of gimmicks, and bad sound and scratchy records.

Needless to say, another puppeteer might have different priorities. In my opinion, however, beginning puppeteers should concentrate on eliminating these top ten mistakes. Eventually, as experience is gained, all the mistakes in the top twenty list should be tackled.

Sinking.

The most common mistake made by beginning puppeteers is letting the puppet sink. Don't do it! Learn to be conscious of how high your puppet is at all times. At first it won't be easy to keep your arm up. Your puppet will start at the right height; but as your show continues, and your arm gets tired, slowly the puppet will appear to be standing in quicksand. Before you know it, all the audience can see is the head. Remember that even though your hand puppet has no legs, in the audience's mind it is standing somewhere. Therefore, the length of the puppets imaginary legs must remain constant.

Some puppeteers like to use an elbow rest a few inches below the playboard. I don't recommend such a device because the puppets on stage tend to become rooted in place by the elbow. The result is that the audience sees two puppets pop up and hardly ever move from their original spots. If, however, the stage is designed primarily for the use of children, an aid to keep the puppet from sinking might be a good idea. It's really a case of the lesser of two evils. If the choice is between seeing puppet statues or just puppet heads, I'd choose the statues. At least the whole puppet would be visible. From that point, action can be choreographed into the production by the teacher or director. On the other hand, nothing can improve the manipulation if all that's visible is a head.

A piece of tape on the sleeve of the puppet can be a handy marker. In an instant, you can check to see if you've got the puppet at the right height. This is particularly useful when moving the puppet from side to side. Everyone has a tendency to move the arm in an arc radiating from the elbow—but the result of the movement is that the puppet is lower at the extreme ends of the arc. Instead, your elbow must move with your arm. A marker will let you know if you've done this movement adequately.

Probably the hardest time to keep the puppet's height constant is when you move from the playboard toward the background. In this case, you must allow for the sightline of the audience—which means you must gradually raise the puppet as you move upstage toward the scenery. If you stay at the playboard level when you move upstage, your audience will see a puppet that appears to be sinking even though you keep it perfectly horizontal. Correcting for the sightline is very difficult because of the many variables you must consider, such as the size and height of your audience and the depth of your stage. Only practice, and a director in the audience when you rehearse, can help you master this technique.

Breaking Character.

Breaking character is a sin that all actors, including puppeteers, must avoid. The voice that you invent for a puppet identifies the personality of that character. The unique qualities of that particular voice characterization must remain consistent throughout the show.

The voice can't begin to change halfway through the performance. Under no circumstances should the audience ever hear a giggle or a whisper in your real voice. It's all right to cough or sneeze, provided the puppet appears to be doing so. In fact, such occurrences provide so much realism and believability for your character that you might even want to work a burp or a sneeze into the show.

The ability to adlib when the unexpected happens is a true sign of showmanship. You must fully understand the way the character you've created would react to any given situation. There should be no noticeable difference in the voice or personality just because something happens that is not in the script. If you forget a line, think of anything to keep the action going. Don't leave your puppet sitting there speechless. Have it complain about an urge to sneeze. If a fellow puppeteer forgets a line, help him out. Anything goes—provided you stay in character. Don't begin to whisper to the fellow standing next to you backstage. Instead, have the puppet do the talking: either puppet to puppet to puppeteer. You might even bring the audience into the action. Maybe someone in the audience can remember how the story goes, or possibly there's a doctor in the house to relieve the puppet's instant attack of tennis elbow. Hopefully, after improvising your way through the dilemma you'll be able to pick up on your story somewhere and continue. If you've stayed in character, the audience will have no real way of knowing that your hi-jinks weren't preplanned and well-rehearsed.

Weak Voice Projection.

Nothing is more irritating to an audience than to be able to hear only 50 percent of what is being said. If your voice projection is weak, do one of two things: mike your show or work on louder projection. You must mike large public performances unless you have an incredibly loud, well-trained voice. But for the most part, smaller shows held in intimate surroundings don't need to be miked. Just speak up, and keep your face pointed in the direction of the puppet when delivering your lines. This will aim your voice up and over the wall. You should be watching your puppet most of the time anyway. Remember not to become distracted and look somewhere else when you're speaking. You should look for props (or whatever) ahead of time, while someone else is speaking. Otherwise you'll be throwing your voice backstage as you look around, and it will be absorbed by the wall created by the stage.

Most beginning puppeteers don't understand that you must speak much louder than you would think. You are behind a wall, and you must compensate for this. You cannot speak the way you would when addressing a crowd from a podium. Don't worry because you sound as if you're on the verge of shouting to your fellow puppeteers. It will sound fine to the audience. If you're doing it right, they won't even be aware of how hard you tried. They will be aware only that your total show was polished. They may not know why the production was so entertaining, but you'll know that the absence of technical difficulties helped to make it professional.

Although it is important to speak as loudly as possible, be careful that you don't strain your voice. Some crazy voices can ruin your vocal chords when you try to do them loudly. Voice volume should be supported from low in your chest, not in your neck and throat. Unless you've had previous experience with voice projection, you might consider taking singing lessons. The basic principles of diaphragm control are the same. In any case, improvement of your voice projection should be one of your goals as a beginning puppeteer.

Poor Diction.

Speaking clearly is as important as speaking loudly. It is easy to get so keyed up in your first performing experiences that you speak too quickly. Even though you have a lot on your mind, you can't overlook your diction when you're performing. You must make an extra effort to speak slowly. When you do, you are less likely to run words together. To make sure your diction is good, have someone sit out front and listen to your rehearsal. I know that it is hard to imagine, as you read this, how bad your diction can become. Often, when you've gone over the material countless times in rehearsal, you can lose the signficance of what you're saying. But your audience will be hearing the words for the first time. You may know the story and dialogue by heart, but the audience must be able to follow the story by piecing together the action and the words as they hear and see them. Each passage will be important to them; so pay attention to your entire dialogue, no matter how repetitious a passage may become in rehearsal.

A good way to approach diction practice is to think of the way you would speak to a deaf person. When you have to shout in someone's ear, you say each word separately and you stress the final consonants. Now I'm not suggesting you deliver your lines v-e-r-y s-l-o-w-l-y, but the basic idea is the same. People naturally compensate for their lazy speech when they speak to their deaf grandfathers. The challenge for you, delivering your lines in a puppet show, is to get your dialogue to sound natural while you concentrate on good diction. You don't want to be too exaggerated in your speech, but you should try not to drop the final consonants of words.

Be aware of what's happening to your speech. You should be projecting the words out of your mouth, over the stage, and to the audience. Your whole face should be involved with putting life and clarity into your words. The audience may not see your expressions, but your voice will transmit them if you're really feeling your part. Your whole body must become involved with the character to provide real emotion behind your voice.

Finally, don't let the level of your delivery trail off at the end of a passage. Just as you should not drop the final consonants of words, you should not swallow the final words of a sentence. Your first words should have the same volume as your last.

Out of Sync Movement.

There are several ways in which your stage movements can be out of sync. With hand puppets that don't have mouths, your manipulation must follow the "freeze principle." This is a way to guarantee that the audience understands which puppet is supposed to be talking. If it's not your turn to speak, your puppet should stand still. Only the puppet that's speaking should be moving; when it's done, it should "freeze" in place while the next one speaks. This principle does not require your puppet to become a complete statue, however. You can move slightly in reaction to what the other guy is saying, to suggest that you're listening. But be careful not to overdo it; if two puppets are moving at the same time, the audience can become confused.

If your puppets have mouths not only must you follow the freeze principle, but when it is your turn to speak the mouth must move in time with the words. Good lip-sync is important because it adds a lot of realism and believability to the character. Jim Henson's Muppets are a notable example. Their lip-sync is consistently excellent because Henson feels its importance so strongly. A notable exception to this rule, however, is the mouth on Burr Tillstrom's Olliver J. Dragon, which moves only roughly in sync with the words. Yet his performance never seems to lack because of this. He can get away with it because Ollie is so strong and believable a character that you never even notice. Still the consensus among the pros is that if your puppet has a mouth it should move in sync.

A novice puppeteer should try to develop movements for a puppet that are appropriate for its character. An old character should move differently from a juvenile character. If the movement does not fit the character, the movement should be considered out of sync.

Wordy Scripts.

> Yak, Yak, Yak (meow) Yak, Yak Yakkety

Too many puppeteers, even those with long track records, fall prey to the evils of wordy scripts. Puppetry is an action medium. This is very important to remember.

Puppets can handle pantomime extremely well. Tell your story with as much pantomime as possible. Use speech only where it is absolutely necessary to further the plot, or to explain what cannot be shown on stage (if possible, show everything on stage at all times).

Admittedly, pantomime is a difficult medium; but to work around its limitations is the challenge for the actor, director, and writer. If the puppets get up on stage and talk, talk, talk, hardly ever moving from their original spots, you're not going to hold audience attention. You have to work in movement, many entrances and exits, and action. You must bring your puppet to life, and the best way to do this is to spend a lot of effort on choreography.

Too many puppeteers try to write and produce shows better suited to other mediums. Clever dialogue may work fine in the legitimate theatre, but scripts intended for the stage can be intensely boring when turned into puppet shows. For this reason, I don't care for puppet productions of Shakespeare or opera. This kind of material is best suited for the medium for which it was intended.

When you're adapting a short story or script to a puppet show, make sure there is enough action in the story to begin with. Some sort of conflict between two puppets (or a puppet and itself) is the minimum requirement. Explore all the dimensions and varieties of the conflict (comic and tragic), and then resolve the conflict. This is the essence of drama, the essence of theatre, and the essence of puppetry.

You may not want to get into violence, but slapstick traditionally has worked well with puppets. The popularity of Punch and Judy owes a lot to the fight scenes. How dull Punch and Judy would be if all they did was get up and talk. Action is what the audience has come to see—not puppet statues with big mouths. You must search for a wide range of movements and moods you can portray with your puppet. Don't rely on the voice of the puppet too much, even though the voice does a lot to identify the character of the puppet. Instead of words, it should be the actions, reactions, and tone of voice of the puppet that lets the audience know what he's thinking. Puppets speak a universal language appreciated by people of all ages when approached this way. Don't be afraid to chop the traditional story line of a tale to pieces, if this will give you more action and fewer words.

Complicated Plot.

Your script should be easy for the audience to follow. The simpler the story line, the younger the age group to which you can play. Your production should have charm and sophistication for the adults, and (at the same time) simplicity for the children. In my opinion, the best puppet shows have universal appeal. This is not to say that you can't gear your production primarily to a specific age group. If you know your audience will be mostly first and second graders, you ought to have a lot of slapstick and clowning around. However, don't forget that there will be adults watching too. Occasionally, throw in a remark intended for them.

A puppet show meant primarily for adults will be appreciated more by children than you might think, provided the plot isn't too complicated to follow. If the plot is so complicated that even the adults have trouble keeping the story straight, you have more the makings of a novel than of a puppet show.

An uncomplicated plot doesn't have to be boring or uneventful. There should be one main goal that your characters are trying to accomplish. You don't want the audience to forget it, so find excuses throughout the show to repeat it. Each time a new character comes along the mission is explained to him. A perfect example is Dorothy, on her way to meet the Wizard of Oz. Within this plot are many subplots, such as why the other characters want to meet the Wizard and the numerous conflicts which they have to overcome to keep on. As long as there's unity to the story, and the audience knows at any given moment what's happening and why, you'll be safe. It's a good idea to have people who haven't seen your production watch a rehearsal. This test preview can help you find out if there are any confusing parts in your story. Schedule this preview as soon as your production is in a presentable form. If you wait until your dress rehearsal, it will be too late to make changes based on the criticisms and suggestions.

A relatively simple plot goes hand in hand with keeping the words to a minimum. If the story is so involved that a lot of dialogue is required to explain the events, you'd be better off choosing a new story. If you are a beginning puppeteer, I strongly suggest you choose traditional folk tales rather than writing your own stories. After you've had some performing experience you will have a feeling for what will work and what won't. This will help you write your own plays. Furthermore, the tried and true stories are good for attracting audiences—and half the battle of keeping the audience up with the story line is won if the audience is already familiar with the story.

Poor Eye Contact.

The ability to control where the puppet appears to be looking is extremely important. Too often beginning puppeteers (and experienced puppeteers) lack control of the puppet's eye contact. This is usually attributable to an error in manipulation and a design flaw.

Well-designed eyes have a definite point of focus. To the audience, the character is looking, and therefore is alive and thinking. If the puppet has only a vague and rather blank stare, there's little that good manipulation will be able to do. However, even a puppet with excellent focus must be properly handled. When you want the puppet to look at the audience, the audience should feel it's being watched. When the puppet sees something on stage that startles him, we should know what the puppet is looking at.

Ask for coaching; practice to become familiar with the unique focus of each one of your puppets. Learn the difference between a glance above and beyond the audience, and a glance directly at the people or at a particular object.

Scene Changes: Too Long and Too Many.

Television audiences of today are used to fast-paced action and instantaneous scene changes. It's important to remember that your audience has become spoiled in this regard. Don't take a long time to change the scenery, and don't plan too many scenes. A long scene change will make your audience restless and bored. If you're constantly stopping the action to change to a new setting you will annoy your audience, especially if there is a long wait until the action resumes.

Once you realize the importance of a fast scene change, you should try in as many ways as possible to speed up the changes. Equipment that works efficiently is very important. Whoever is to handle the scenery should practice with it and try to discover all the things that might possibly go wrong during a scene change. Measures should be taken to prevent these technical foul-ups from happening. Finally, more practice is required. When more than one person is to be responsible for the change, they must practice together. This team should operate like a well-lubricated, finely-tuned machine—not like a panic stricken, uncoordinated group of Keystone Cops. Every move must be choreographed, so that persons are in the right place at the right time or out of the way when scene pieces are being moved. When every move backstage is rehearsed, a troupe of puppeteers can cut the time required to do each change by at least half.

The solo puppeteer is at a real disadvantage when it comes to executing scene changes quickly. One moment you're a puppeteer; then you must put down the puppets, close the curtain and/or change the lighting, remove the old scene, put up the new one, open the curtain and lights, and resume the show. Probably the best solution is that of master soloist Dick Myers: make the scene change an entertaining part of the show. He holds audience attention by letting them watch the silhouettes of the scenery being changed. Remember: most people are spellbound when they are allowed to peek backstage. There is something mysterious about the backstage equipment that helps create the magical illusion of drama. When you let your audience watch your scene change, you're playing off this emotion. However, you must be very careful not to destroy the fantasy world the puppets have created.

Poor Finale.

The end of your show should bring the whole production together
with flair. Nothing is worse than to treat your audience to a lively,
entertaining show, and then to let them down at the end. The show
should not just stop; it should come to an end—a finale. Your finale is
what your audience will remember most when they leave the theatre. If
you have created a great impression all along, don't spoil it with a
poor finale.

A good finale is the earmark of a professional production. It should
stir up a spine-tingling frenzy in your audience. The stage is lit as
brightly as possible, the action is quick, the sound is at its peak—and
then it's over. If you've hit the magical combination right, the audience
instantly breaks into applause. It's no accident when it happens. A
professional show primes the audience for the exact moment of its
ending. If you've had them on the edge of their seats all along, they
should jump to their feet when the curtain comes down.

Don't confuse the finale with the climax of your plot. The climax
should come just *before* the end. All the conflicts have been resolved,
the villian disposed of (or rehabilitated), and all is well again. This is
the perfect time to break into a song. A musical finale is most popular
because it's the easiest, and perhaps the most effective. If possible,
your entire cast should appear on stage to sing. This may require the

extra hands of your technicians—except for one, who must coordinate the lighting blackout and/or curtain with the last note of your song.

The end of your show should be given careful consideration from the first moment the production is conceived. Throughout the process of writing the story, you must know where and how the show will end. If you let it go, and write your script without the knowledge of how it will end, you may have trouble figuring out an appropriate finale. Many beginning puppeteers underestimate the importance of a strong finale and make this mistake.

I would like to point out one more thing that comes at the end of the show and is often overlooked: the curtain call. After the finale, while the audience is still applauding, the troupe of puppeteers should come out (smiling) and bow to the audience. To keep your production professional from start to finish, this curtain call too should be rehearsed. You should know from which side and in what order you will appear, and you should have a signal so that you bow together. Each of you should count a predetermined number of beats, so that you rise in unison also. As you leave the stage together, keep smiling even though you're dead tired. You will give the audience the distinct impression that you are a tight professional troupe that likes your work. These considerations may seem small, but they are all part of the polish that makes the difference between the professional and the amateur.

Chapter 5

Tips From The Pros

Many professional puppeteers have contributed their knowledge to make this chapter possible. All were asked to complete the unfinished sentences as briefly as possible; therefore, an abbreviated response is indicative of an attempt to comply with the request, not of limited knowledge. These pros somehow found time in their very busy schedules to give their best advice to beginning puppeteers.

The questions were interpreted in many different ways, partly because they are very general questions, but also because this group of people represents a wide variety of artistic approaches. No one answer is right or wrong, or better than the rest. Each has something profound and important to reveal to the novice puppeteer. Years of practical experience, trial and error, and dedication have lead each of these puppeteers to approach the art in his own particular way. Nevertheless, a certain unity will become evident to you as you read their responses. Although they may have different things to say, the answers all point in the same general direction.

I especially want to note that this list is not an attempt to pick the best living puppeteers. Many notable and brilliant persons are not included, due to space limitations and to the fact that not every puppeteer queried responded to the questionnaire.

I hope you find these comments as interesting as I do. I am pleased to note that they are consistent with the advice I have given you. Reading these tips should help you crystallize in your mind the essential points I have stressed throughout this book.

Paul Ashley, New Rochelle, New York.

Paul is perhaps best known for his years of television work with Chuck McCann. His puppet caricatures of famous personalities are also highly acclaimed.

A beginning puppeteer should have dedication, great imagination, and the ability to create and construct all his concepts, except for very large productions where he might dictate his aims and desired effect.

The goal of a puppeteer is limited primarily by his desires, whether far-reaching or immediate. Accomplishment should be the net result.

When performing, you should avoid breaking concentration.

The performability of a good puppet is based on its limitations and capacity for its intended purpose.

A good puppet stage should be put together considering all the necessary physical and theatrical aspects, not forgetting the necessity of a flexible accessible working area.

When rehearsing it's a good idea to make positive and clear intent of purpose and emphasis. Consider all technical, audio, acting, special effects, special business, etc. that go into stimulating a good performance.

Is there anything in the puppet world that really bugs you? My beefs in the puppet world are the following: great lack of good craftsmen in construction and design; lack of good material concepts; the idea that puppet shows are designed for preschool children only, when in fact they should involve and entice a general audience from four to eighty.

Joe Ayers, Johnson City, New York.

When Joe isn't dreaming up novel puppet entertainments, he works as an advisory engineer for IBM, designing the logic for aerospace computers. His shows use a projected shadow technique he has pioneered, and are mainly adult oriented.

A beginning puppeteer should study everyone about him. He should note the features and mannerisms that make each person and individual a "character." In this way he learns how to create a puppet character of the desired personality with a minimum of fussiness in the making, and a minimum of gestures in the manipulation. Learn to project your puppet's character with only the essential gestures or mannerisms.

The goal of a puppeteer is to make his audience "suspend reality" for a little while; to forget they are watching puppets, and enter into the spirit of the performance. The ability to do this separates the puppeteers from the mechanics.

When performing you should avoid sneezing at inappropriate times.

The performability of a good puppet is based on making it as flexible as its form permits. My finest puppet is a dragon, cut from foam rubber with a head of plastic wood. He is about four feet long. One rod is attached to his movable jaw, the other his thorax, between his front legs. Using only these two rods and the natural bounce of the foam rubber, an amazing amount of movement and control is possible.

A good puppet stage should be comfortable for the puppeteer and for the audience. Remember that you will have to play in many different environments. Make your stage flexible to adapt to changing sight lines. Arrange your stage so that you never have to stay in a cramped position for an extended period of time. Avoid blinding the audience with unmasked lighting equipment.

When rehearsing, it's a good idea to rig up a mirror where you can see the action of the puppets, and run a tape recorder to catch the voices and comments for later discussion. The mirror shows a completely different performance from the one I'm seeing on the other side of the footlights.

Is there anything in the puppet world that really bugs you? Yes, certain rather amateur "professionals" with an exaggerated estimation of their artistry. The really great artists play down their own triumphs and give generously of their knowledge and experience to the new generation of puppeteers. The others should be made a "source of innocent merriment." All prosy and dull puppet performers whose offerings falter and bore, shall be forced to witness their own performances daily from nine to four (with a profound bow to W. S. Gilbert).

Bil Baird, New York City.

Bil has been a puppeteer since the age of seven. He was an early associate of the great Tony Sarg. For the past forty years he has run his own shows, and is now one of the most respected authorities in the world of puppetry.

A beginning puppeteer should consider that pantomime is the most important thing. I consider the action of the script the most important thing. The next thing is the looks of the puppet, and the third thing is the dialogue—in that order. Other people may not work that way, but I have to think that way. Oftentimes puppeteers start because they're good at sculpture, and they make themselves a beautiful puppet and don't know what to do with it. There are several professional puppeteers who are limping around today because they don't know what to do with their puppets. I think the impact on the audience is what they should consider.

The goal of a puppeteer is to fulfill himself, I suppose; and to have fun doing it. Don't get into it if you don't like it. Don't get into it just for money. You're creating a sort of life—an imaginative and different life—and the more successful you are at creating it, the happier you and the audience will be. On top of this, the nearer you are to real life—looking like people and acting like people—the more unsuccessful you will be. Puppets have a look of their own and an action of their own, and that's one reason animal puppets are so successful. If they're far out and still comment on life, I think they're successful; but if you try to make little people, forget it.

When performing, you should avoid . . . I could write a book on this, but one thing to avoid is talking too much and depending on lip-sync rather than the action of the whole body.

The performability of a good puppet is based on action, to the limit of what the puppet can do, instead of being hindered and stiff. Lean in the direction of extreme action: just because a frog has a thick neck doesn't mean it can't turn.

A good puppet stage should bring out the best there is in the puppet and, to a certain extent, divorce him from his operator.

When rehearsing, it's a good idea to rehearse more than you think is necessary.

Is there anything in the puppet world that really bugs you? Yeah, but I'm not going to tell you.

Frank Ballard, Storrs, Connecticut.

A past president of The Puppeteers of America, Frank has a puppetry study program affiliated with the Drama Department of The University of Connecticut, the only college or university in the United States where you can major in Puppetry.

A beginning puppeteer should seek a thorough training in all aspects of theatre.

The goal of a puppeteer is to give his audiences the very best in quality puppet theatre.

When performing you should avoid sloppy showmanship.

The performability of a good puppet is based on good design and construction and a well-rehearsed puppeteer.

A good puppet stage should be functional and not ostentatious. It should call attention to the puppets and not to itself.

When rehearsing, it's a good idea to . . . it's imperative that there be a director; someone who can sit out front and observe what the performance will look like from the audience point of view.

Is there anything in the puppet world that really bugs you? Yes! The dozens of people who call themselves "puppeteers," but who really only dabble in puppetry for their own amusement. These individuals have neither the interest nor the know-how to better the quality of their shows, and do a great deal of harm by furthering poor puppetry.

Richard Bradshaw, Kensington, Australia.

A solo shadow puppeteer of international fame, Richard is able to accomplish everything puppet theatre should accomplish using only the barest essentials. His performances were honored with standing ovations at both the 1972 and 1974 Puppeteers of America Festivals.

A beginning puppeteer should choose a particular, simple way of animating a simple puppet—strings, hand (inside or out), rods, magnets, whatever—and then try to devise small plays with similiar simple figures, expanding from there. I have always found it valuable to put severe limitations on myself to start with, and then try to find a direction to move in. I get confused if too many directions are offered.

The goal of a puppeteer is to fascinate the audience by diverting attention away from the puppeteer himself to an object under his control. For many, the aim is to make an object which is actually subject to external forces appear to be moved by internal (physical and emotional) forces.

When performing, you should avoid appearing to be out of control of yourself, the puppets, or the audience. A puppeteer is one who controls; a good puppeteer appears to be in control of everything.

The performability of a good puppet is based on . . . A good puppet is one over which the puppeteer can have a high degree of control. It does what he wants, when he wants. It does not have unpredictable behavior (such as joints that stick).

A good puppet stage should be functional. It should not deprive the puppets of impact by either inhibiting their movement or distracting the attention of the audience. This doesn't mean I'm against strongly decorated stages. There are times when such decoration can set the mood or enhance the mood of the drama.

When rehearsing, it's a good idea to work through the action at a deliberately slow pace at first, mastering the difficult actions slowly. Invite in a rehearsal audience at some point to test your timing. Aim to please yourself, as if you were able to sit out front. I try not to do things I wouldn't enjoy.

Is there anything in the puppet world that really bugs you? Lots of things in the puppet world bug me. I am bugged by boring shows (i.e. most puppet shows), especially when they are pretentious ("arty") as well as boring.

I am bugged by bad puppeteers and bad showmen who think they are good and have giant egos. (I have admiration for bad puppeteers who are nevertheless good showmen.)

I am bugged by puppeteers who give nothing of themselves in shows. This is expecially true of the many people who copy other puppeteers, or copy from books without adding anything original.

Steve Brezzo, La Jolla, California.

Steve was the first American to receive a Master of Fine Arts degree in Puppetry from the University of Connecticut. He is now active in puppetry at the La Jolla Museum of Contemporary Art.

A beginning puppeteer should . . . I suppose a good notion for any beginning puppet artist is the recognition of the limited financial attributes of his career. Even assuming that few artists enter an esthetic career with a profit motive in mind, he should still be aware of the fact that this is not a big money business, and that much of his time will be spent simply selling his product to a public long content with *Sleeping Beauty* and *Jack and the Beanstalk.* He should also force himself not to set his style into a formalized pattern that will both limit his creativity and be inflexible in its artistic potential. This is no easy thing, for popular tastes often lead us in directions of reproduction without a philosophical basis—how many Muppets must we see? Our society generally regards invalid an esthetic undertaking which in its eyes is not cute, "utilitarian" or representational (as opposed to abstract). This is a hard fact of life for any artist setting out to experiment and create new boundaries for his art, but it must be recognized and considered by any novice puppeteer.

The goal of a puppeteer is somewhere between a life spent in creative esthetic endeavors and feeding his family at the same time he makes his car payments. Seriously though, his goal should be the synthesis of the various artistic components inherent in his art to a level of fresh and unique theatrical presentation which could be better expressed by no other art form.

When performing, you should avoid cliches, cuteness, repetition, unnecessary action or dialogue, your ego.

The performability of a good puppet is based on movement, characterization, and its "idea."

A good puppet stage should allow the audience to comfortably view the action—nothing more.

This Muppet-like puppet is an excellent prop handler because a human hand is right inside the puppet's glove. This character, Davey Simpson, is used by Ralph Kalatucka and Earl Kress primarily for educational television skits.
Photo by Tom Kervitsky, Courtesy of Earl Kress, Levittown, Pa.

Aztec ice skater Marionette, by Rucy Gayton. Fred Cowan Puppets, Crawfordsville, Indiana.

Two characters form Daniel Llords' The Firebird. The hollow heads symbolize that these were once beautiful maidens, but are now without faces because they are without souls.
Courtesy Daniel Llords.

Performances of The Bread and Puppet Theatre seem visually grotesque to some people. It's all part of Peter Schuman's dedication to remaining close to the masque origins of puppetry. This scene is the 1967 production, The Dead Man Rises.
Photo by Robert Alazvakì, Courtesy Mrs. Peter Schuman, Plainfield, Vt.

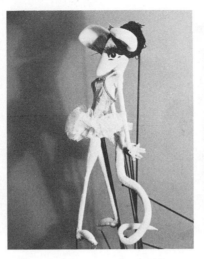

Sonya, by Alan Stevens, 1972, The Smithsonian Puppet Theatre. Photo by Harry Bagdasian, courtesy Alan Stevens

Miss Annabella Squeek is the Prima Ballerina of the Frog Print Theatre, created by Robert and Nikki Tilroe of Ontario, Canada. The Tilroes perform on Canadian television.
Courtesy Ken McKay

Queen Bruinhilda and Cora Castlemouse in the Christmas play Little Red Rocking Chair by Tom Tichenor. Photo by William M. King, courtesy Tom Tichenor.

Here are two classic opposites for whom you should be able easily to invent voices: Alice (sweet and innocent), and the Queen of Hearts (mean and stuck-up). These rod puppets, by Ken Moses, are from the Pickwick Puppet Production Alice in Wonderland.
Courtesy Ken Moses, Fairview, NJ.

This plastic wood rod puppet by Dick Myers is a speciality puppet, designed only to play the guitar. This character is so believable and convincing that the audience sees the puppet tap its foot while it plays although the foot is attached in a fixed position and cannot move.
Courtesy Dick Myers, Hyde Park, NY.

A hand is helpful in adding expression to a puppet with a mouth. As Jerry Halliday demonstrates here, his puppet is constructed in two pieces. When he's behind the playboard during a show, the audience assumes the two are attached.
Courtesy Jerry Halliday, Norfolk, Va.

These wooden cutouts are a simple and effective way to get a horse and carriage on a puppet stage. (From The Wind in the Willows, by Mr. Badger's Traveling Repertory Company.)
Courtesy Kathryn Arrigon, NYC.

These puppets, by Paul Ashley of New Rochelle, N.Y., not only look like caricatures of Sammy Davis and Flip Wilson, but their body movements and voices also resemble the real thing.
Courtesy Paul Ashley

The author in a television studio at Ithaca College. The microphone is taped to my shirt so that it will not bounce around and get in the way.
Courtesy Jonathan Silverman

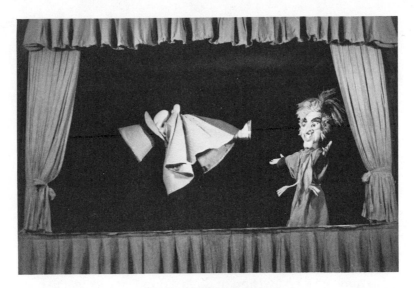

The black background hides Paul Ashley's black sleeve.
Courtesy Paul Ashley, New Rochelle, NY.

Small-scale educational productions are fun not only for audiences of all ages, but fun for the puppeteers as well. Seen here, left to right, are Jim, and Grace Berlin (kneeling) and Roger Sharp, Barbara Echols, Gaye Sharp and Clay Foster (standing).

Photo by Fred Miller, Courtesy of Gracie Berlin and The Puppets of God, Stillwater, Okla.

When rehearsing, it's a good idea to demand discipline and aim for nothing less than perfect art.

Is there anything in the puppet world that really bugs you? The almost instinctive categorization of puppetry as a "craft," or exclusively child-oriented art form.

Bruce Chesse, Walnut Creek, California.

Bruce is the son of puppeteer Ralph Chesse, and has been in puppetry since he was a small boy. He now teaches foam puppet workshops in colleges and civic centers, and is also an active puppeteer.

A beginning puppeteer should find or build a puppet and put it to use. Recognize your strengths and weaknesses and put them to work for you.

The goal of a puppeteer is to find the particular technique that works for you and to explore it fully. Your objective should be to communicate not only with yourself but with the audience. Know what it is that you want to communicate and do it.

When performing, you should avoid self-indulgence.

The performability of a good puppet is based on your relationship to it and what it has to say and do for you.

A good puppet stage should function according to your needs. Different puppets dictate different stages. Some dictate none at all.

When rehearsing, it's a good idea to experiment. The rehearsal is the place for that. Your next step to simplify what you have put together, weeding out the unnecessary. You never need as much as you think you need. Economy of movement and dialogue are the hardest things to learn. Rehearse with an audience at least once.

Is there anything in the puppet world that really bugs you? The idea, entertained by so many, that talent should be sought out to the exclusion of those whose skills are yet to be developed. It is important to recognize individual abilities. Everyone has a skill of some kind. In teaching, it is the job of the teacher to find and develop it.

Larry Engler, Roslyn Heights, New York.

Poko Puppets is the combined effort of Virginia Lloyd-Davies and Larry Engler. He is currently the president of the Puppetry Guild of Greater New York, and co-author (with Carol Fijan) of the book *Making Puppets Come Alive.*

A beginning puppeteer should realize that he is a beginner. In a phrase, keep it simple. Realize your limitations, and make them work for you (i.e., emphasize what you do best).

The goal of a puppeteer to communicate; to express one's ideas clearly and communicate them to an audience. It is a *performing* art. Hopefully, the puppeteer will also entertain his audience. I hope that he will do more than that, but at least that. Please note that to entertain does not necessarily mean to be humorous—I find *Death of a Salesman* very entertaining.

When performing, you should avoid allowing your own ego to take over the puppet. The audience should not be aware of you operating a puppet, but merely of the puppet's character. I have observed two flaws in almost every puppet production I have seen; too much talk, and too little humor. I hope that puppeteers will also avoid too much movement (every movement should have a meaning, as should every word of a script).

The performability of a good puppet is based on how effectively it can be brought to life. Can it physically do the actions required in the script. (i.e., pick up a cup, fall down, fly, eat cookies, and so on).

A good puppet stage should function for the purpose for which it is being used. If it is a touring stage it should be light, easy to set up and take down, attractive, and functional. The stage should not detract from the performance. I like stages to look simple and neat.

When rehearsing, it's a good idea to rehearse! Ideally, one should have a separate director who can watch from the front and direct from the front, without having to run back and manipulate the puppets as well. Take it step by step. Start with just the movement of a scene, then the voice and character (perhaps done best through improvisation), then situation and script. There is no one way to rehearse, as indeed one cannot generalize for any phase of an art form. As with all aspects of puppetry—absorb what knowledge you can, then experiment to determine what works best for you.

Is there anything in the puppet world that really bugs you? One thing that distresses me is the petty, close-minded nature of many of the people in the business. In the many other art forms (e.g., jazz music), there seems to be more feeling of camaraderie, let's-get-together-and-create-something-beautiful rather than it's a secret! I am also bugged by the amount of rotten puppetry I see by so-called professionals, who think themselves beyond criticism in their perfection of the art. I wish that more puppeteers could take as well as give positive, constructive criticism. This, I feel, is the only way that we can establish a standard for the art form and elevate it beyond the novelty category.

Carol Fijan and Paul Vincent-Davis, Great Neck, New York.
Carol and Paul are co-directors of The National Theatre of Puppet Arts, which was founded in 1969 in Great Neck, New York. Carol is an internationally known puppeteer, lecturer, actress, teacher, author, and former board member of the Puppeteers of America.

A beginning puppeteer should be a trained actor.

The goal of a puppeteer is to communicate an idea through his instrument (the puppet) to an audience.

When performing, you should avoid showing off. It is the puppet who is the star, not the puppeteer.

The performability of a good puppet is based on proper design concepts.

A good puppet stage should be a functional part of the play.

When rehearsing, it's a good idea to have an outside director.

Is there anything in the puppet world that really bugs you? The emphasis of most puppeteers on the artsy-craftsy aspect of puppetry, rather than on the performing aspect.

Jim Gamble, Rancho Palos Verdes, California.

In addition to an average of 300 performances a year, Jim is a fulltime airline pilot, flying a Boeing 727 for Continental Airlines. He is able to perform easily across the country, as well as in Europe, South America, the Middle East, and the South Pacific.

A beginning puppeteer should experiment with as many types and styles of puppetry as he can.

The goal of a puppeteer is first, to entertain or inspire his audience; *second* to entertain himself.

When performing, you should tune to your audience. Their feedback is the sole measure of your ability.

The performability of a good puppet is based on movement, character, and ease of manipulation.

A good puppet stage should enhance the play or act, not fight or overshadow it.

When rehearsing, it's a good idea to find an unbiased audience to offer criticism.

Is there anything in the puppet world that really bugs you? Plays that are too wordy; variety acts that are too long; too many beginners who pass themselves off as professionals.

I am writing this high over the Pacific, en route to the mainland after an unhurried, relaxing week on the island of Mani. All my remarks at this point seem of little consequence. But novices must be encouraged—though not applauded unduly, for (especially in the case of novice puppeteers) they seem to develop a great sense of worth and cease to feel the pulse of their audience.

Professionalism is more than simply charging money for your shows; is more than earning your living with puppets. It implies a high standard toward which you can strive and by which your work can be measured. I believe puppeteers should strive toward professionalism through experimenting, freely exchanging ideas, and embracing other, nonperforming arts (sculpture, painting, engineering, electronics, and so on). So many disciplines can embrace puppetry, if only we would take the time to investigate.

Steve Hansen, New York City.

Steve is best known for his street performances of Punch and Judy. He has performed on numerous local news and talk shows, with Jim Henson's Muppets, Bil Baird's Marionettes, and Bob Brown's Marionettes.

A beginning puppeteer should get as liberal an education as possible; see as much puppetry and theatre as possible; study theatre, dance, sculpture, set design, directing, and so on.

The goal of a puppeteer is to think of himself as an artist. He must try to express himself the best he can through the medium.

When performing, you should avoid big trucks and dark corridors.

The performability of a good puppet is based on Newton's Second Law of Motion.

A good puppet stage should not fall down.

When rehearsing, it's a good idea to salute the flag.

Is there anything in the puppet world that really bugs you? Yes, Most puppet shows. Puppeteers must know that what they do is a very complex art. Most people in America have come to relate to a puppet show as an amusement for children; unfortunately, so do many puppeteers. Anyone considering the art of puppetry should remember that even though puppetry requires many diverse skills, puppetry is a theatre art. It must be entertaining. You can have the most beautiful puppets and sets in the world, but if you can't be entertaining with them you should put them in a museum.

John and Allelu Kurten, Hyde Park, New York.

The Kurten's chief interests are satire and simplicity of means. John teaches drama at Vassar College; Allelu is a board member of the Puppeteers of America.

A beginning puppeteer should avoid How-to-do-it books. He should first discover what he's trying to do for his audience by way of expression and movement, because this can lead him to a creative puppetry that is personal and his own, rather than the stereotypes produced in books and courses. We discovered that tennis balls and wooden dowels were ideally suited to our type of satire, and that audiences enjoy the economy of form and expression. Too many puppets do nothing and say nothing (even when gloriously created), and so fall into the category of handicrafts.

The goal of a puppeteer is to express, through the mediums of form, movement, and sound, his responses to life—whether humorous, tragic, or satiric—and to concentrate, clarify, and project this to his audience.

When performing, you should avoid bad tape, poor lighting, excessive length, lack of self-criticism, and cluttered visual images.

The performability of a good puppet is based on ease of movement and the appropriateness of its design to the flow and content of the particular show (the music, dialogue, and overall concept).

A good puppet stage should be light, simple, and—*please*—carefully designed so that the masking area does not detract from the playing space. Avoid reflective fabrics and designs, that call attention to themselves.

When rehearsing, it's a good idea to put yourself in the audience's place and be brutally self-critical. Be sure that the show is clear and projects over a distance. Get an honest critic to tell you the truth.

Is there anything in the puppet would that really bugs you? Self-Indulgence—The self-indulgence of considering everything one makes as a valid form of art and/or puppetry, when in reality the vast majority is cute rubbish.

Ken Moses, Fairview, New Jersey.

Ken is currently director of the Pickwick Puppet Theatre. He is also the sound and light advisor for the Puppeteers of America. His productions are often presented with full symphony orchestras, and sometimes with rock bands (such as Mott the Hoople).

A beginning puppeteer should avoid attempting something far beyond his or her ability; overextending himself. Keep it simple.

The goal of a puppeteer is the same as that of any artist to reach and touch his audience.

When performing, you should avoid too much clutter backstage.

The performability of a good puppet is based on the puppeteer's ability more than the puppet. A good puppeteer can make anything work well.

A good puppet stage should set up and pack fast; be sturdy, lightweight, low in cost, easy to repair, adaptable, and unobtrusive.

When rehearsing it's a good idea to keep track of how the show looks from the front; turn off the phone; keep snacks handy; take breaks.

Is there anything in the puppet world that really bugs you? People who think it's an easy way to make a living.

Mike Oznowicz, Oakland, California.

Mike is the current president of the Puppeteers of America. He has been active with puppetry and the P. of A. for many years.

A beginning puppeteer should be very patient learning his craft.

The goal of a puppeteer is to entertain in good taste!

When performing, you should avoid lengthy, talk-talk shows.

The performability of a good puppet is based on good craftsmanship.

A good puppet stage should be *pleasantly* visible.

When rehearsing it's a good idea to rehearse a lot!

Is there anything in the puppet world that really bugs you? People who did not make it in the theatre, and are hiding behind the puppet medium.

Margo Rose, Waterford, Connecticut.

It is said among the members of the Puppeteers of America that no two people have given so much for so many years as Margo and Rufus Rose. Not only have they created hundreds of beautiful marionettes (including Howdy Doody), but they have given kind advice, constructive criticism, and detailed instruction at festival after festival.

A beginning puppeteer should learn as much about the crafts involved as possible. He should get training in the many areas of the art: script writing, design, acting, voice, sculpture, woodworking, mechanics, electronics, lighting, music, sewing, painting, manipulating puppets; as well as business management, publicity, and booking of shows. Almost no one has all these talents; he must enlist the aid of those who have the talents he lacks.

The goal of a puppeteer is to entertain.

When performing, you should avoid boring your audience.

The performability of a good puppet is based on a mechanically good puppet and an able puppeteer.

A good puppet stage should be adequate to the needs of the puppeteers and give the audience a good clear view of all that happens.

When rehearsing, it's a good idea to block the show carefully. Memorize the lines; as action is developed memorize every move to be made by both the puppets and puppeteers. Create personalities for the characters by voice and movement. Make the puppets appear to think and feel emotions. Allow rehearsal time for the show to come alive, develop pace, and be fit to show before an audience of your enemies. Adequate rehearsal time for an hour's show would be twelve hours a day every day for two weeks, after all the puppets, scenery, and props are built.

Is there anything in the puppet world that really bugs you? I am bugged by poor showmanship, poor scripts, poor voices, poor manipulation—anything less than excellence. I am particularly bugged by puppeteers who open their curtains and show all to the general public, or invite the general public backstage. What goes on backstage is not the business of the public. The show out front is for the public. Private invitations to puppeteers and aspiring puppeteers to come backstage after the audience has gone are another matter. I am also bugged by audiences rushing backstage as soon as the curtains are closed. It is inconsiderate of puppeteers and of their equipment. One should ask permission and wait until the audience is gone. I am bugged by cute names for puppet companies. Use your own name. Make it famous. Stand up and be counted.

Rufus Rose, Waterford, Connecticut.

It is said among the members of the Puppeteers of America that no two people have given so much fo so many years as Margo and Rufus Rose. Not only have they created hundreds of beautiful marionettes (including Howdy Doody), but they have given kind advice, constructive criticism, and detailed instruction at festival after festival.

A beginning puppeteer should develop character voices. Join the Puppeteers of America; attend the national P. of A. festivals and become involved with the nearest P. of A. guild.

The goal of a puppeteer is to master the art of puppeteering (manipulation) so that the puppet appears to the audience to think. Always improve your art; never be fully satisfied with your accomplished work.

When performing, you should sense the audience response and always leave them wanting more. Play to the last row; be sure that everybody hears and sees everything.

The performability of a good puppet is based on a well-built puppet that can do what the script calls for, and that, through continued practice, behaves with exact timing and grace, avoiding jerkiness and unnecessary movement.

A good puppet stage should be solid and yet light for portability, with a smoothly working front curtain, complete lighting equipment, a high-quality sound system, and an acting area sufficient to give wide action in all directions.

When rehearsing it's a good idea to have a knowledgeable director out front to demand a finished (polished) performance.

Is there anything in the puppet world that bugs you? There are many things in the puppet world that bug me and should bug every puppeteer. Don't love your puppets, but respect them as your acting medium. Be your own severest critic and don't believe half the praise the gushers backstage hand out. Never apologize for your show, but learn from each performance how to improve it. Puppets are not cute. The single most important accomplishment of a good puppeteer is showmanship, utilizing talent.

Tom Tichenor, Nashville, Tennessee.

Tom and his Puppet Playhouse can be found in the story room of the Nashville Public Library. He has performed numerous times on television, and also is the author of his own book on puppetry.

A beginning puppeteer should think and make his puppet think in turn. Puppets should listen to each other, and react to the other puppets. So often puppets on stage behave independently—say their lines, do their jumping around, without regard to the others. Listening with interest, reacting appropriately—these are traits that all puppets should develop.

The goal of a puppeteer is communication. To entertain or educate, you must communicate. A puppeteer has to reach out and touch his audience, to make them care about what he is doing, to make them respond to his puppets. Some performances before live audiences are vital—even if the bulk of your work is television shows in a studio. Live audiences let you know what works and what doesn't, and what reactions different puppet personalities cause. This helps the puppeteer to plan television shows. It is more important to reach the viewers than to get a laugh from the television crew with an inside remark.

When performing, you should avoid letting your mind wander—or you'll suddenly be jolted into reality and find you've missed your cue. The show will die then and there. Keep your energy and interest up. This is especially difficult when doing the same old routines and plays over and over, but most important each performance should be treated as if it is something new and vital. Then the puppets will really come to life.

The performability of a good puppet is based on its believability. The audience must believe in the character, believe it is alive and really breathing. This has nothing to do with its construction or appearance. A good puppeteer can make a bare stick come to life. A bad puppeteer can kill the most beautiful puppet ever made.

A good puppet stage should work. It should fit the particular puppeteer or troupe. What works for one often does not work for another. Usually, simplicity is best. Workability is more important than looks. If the stage has to travel, keep it light. A tired puppeteer finds it difficult to sparkle.

When rehearsing, it's a good idea to let someone hold the puppets up so you can see how the show looks from the audience's view. After the play has been blocked and rehearsed several times, relax and get silly. Do a runthrough. Lose a few inhibitions. We always end up laughing ourselves silly, and usually several really usable ideas pop up. Some of our best stage business has evolved from such sessions—not to mention ad libs that are retained as permanent dialogue. Playing with the puppets is really the only way to get to know them, to learn their individual quirks, shortcomings, and unusual abilities. Very few puppets are perfect. Often their flaws and disabilities can be incorporated into their personalities and characters, adding to them.

Is there anything in the puppet world that really bugs you? Puppets that flop around; puppets that jiggle; puppets that mistake senseless movement for living. Exaggeration is often most effective, but even an exaggerated puppet should have a soul and a personality.

Nikki Tilroe, Ontario, Canada

Nikki and her husband Robert are the creators of the Frog Print Theatre, which produces two to three shows a year and performs on network television in Canada. They have both been guests at Puppeteers of America Festivals as workshop directors and performers.

A beginning puppeteer should be prepared to embark on a continuing quest for expanding personal knowledge and understanding about the theatre in general, about acting, movement, voice control, design, music, and lighting. One needs a healthy respect for the discipline required for the art and the artist to become what is possible to be. Learn everything you can about the craft and the art of puppetry, as well as about related crafts and art forms.

The goal of a puppeteer is to communicate with an audience. The substance of that communication may be ideas, feelings, appreciation, or the sharing of imagination. The puppeteer creates an opportunity for each member of the audience, no matter the age, to experience and share an imagined world.

When performing, you should avoid indulging yourself. You must never forget your audience and their needs to best understand your performance. Always give the audience the best you can give.

The performability of a good puppet is based on knowing what each puppet is supposed to be and do before making or having it made. Then make sure you're well-rehearsed, and clear about what the puppet is doing.

A good puppet stage should make the puppeteer's job easier. It hides what it should hide and shows what it should show. It also adds to and helps create the illusion of the production. It should not distract from or overpower the performance, nor create the impression of being the best thing about the show.

When rehearsing it's a good idea to seek the advice of an out-front director. The director should be responsible for the look and the feeling of the show. When rehearsing, it's important to know everything that you have to do, but also to have an appreciation of how you and your puppet look doing it.

Is there anything in the puppet world that really bugs you? Too many people in the puppet world think they have nothing more to learn, or feel that they can get along well enough with the little skill and training they have. What I find most discouraging is that sometimes people behave as if they don't *want* to spend time and energy developing technique, and don't want to broaden their understanding and experience by collaborating with an experienced puppeteer or puppetry teacher.

Burr Tillstrom, Chicago, Illinois and Saugatuck, Michigan.

Burr is the creator of Kukla, Ollie, and the rest of the Kuklapolitan Players. He is presently artist-in-residence at Hope College's theatre department. He and Fran Allison make occasional television appearances.

A beginning puppeteer should work, work, work. Anywhere you can. Be as broad-based as possible in the arts. Go to plays, opera, dance. Don't think that the puppet is the whole thing, the whole art. A puppet is not art until it is used. It is like the person who wanted to build a violin to play violin music. He first had to build the violin. The puppet is like the violin; it is not art until it is played. Use it and study it.

The goal of a puppeteer is to entertain, communicate ideas, stimulate the imagination of the audience. The more experience he has, the better chance he has of fulfilling that goal.

When performing, you should avoid wearing your audience out. Practice economy. Keep scripts short; edit. Edit performances too. Learn how to pace your performance for contrast. Have quiet moments, as well as big laughs and excitement.

Additional Thoughts: I have always been more theatre-oriented than craft-oriented. In other words, I've always put the least emphasis on the construction of my puppets and the most emphasis on their performance and story—including, of course, manipulation, although manipulation has become more subtle and restrained for me since the advent of television. I think of myself as a storyteller and an actor first; but I consider good puppets, costumes, and sets important also. I like well-made, strong puppets: simple, clean and easy to "read." Costuming and sets should support the performance—complement it—as in any theatrical venture. Music, too, is important in my work.

But the character is always most fascinating to me, and a proper portrayal is only achieved internally—mentally. A puppeteer must be in character just as an actor or a writer becomes subordinate to the part he is playing or creating. Techniques are the mechanics through which an artist sustains and clarifies his creative work, but they are external supplements only and must never become the dominant factor, else creativity disappears and is replaced by construction. I urge a puppeteer to use every chance to perform.

Rod Young, New York City.

As a puppeteer and workshop instructor, Rod gives great emphasis to young people's creativity. His performances are well-known at regional and national puppet festivals.

A beginning puppeteer should see as many shows as possible, read as many books as possible, talk to as many puppeteers as possible, and seek out related arts and study them as well as puppetry. Keep learning and experimenting.

The goal of a puppeteer is to entertain and perhaps educate at the same time; to communicate ideas visually.

When performing, you should avoid boring your audience with self-centered ego trips and stage-waits.

The performability of a good puppet is based on the puppeteer—his thought, voice, personality, and prowess.

A good puppet stage should be designed and lighted with the audience in mind at all times. Visibility is the chief factor.

When rehearsing, it's a good idea to visualize your work or have a director out front. Or use a mirror. Keep surprising yourself as well as your audience.

Is there anything in the puppet world that really bugs you? Nothing or everything. Perhaps the fact that puppetry is too often treated as an unprofessional art form, and too often practiced by nonprofessional performers—for pay.

Peter Zapletal, Jackson, Mississippi.

Peter is puppetry producer for the Mississippi Authority for Educational Television. Prior to coming to the United States from Czechoslovakia, he received a degree in puppetry from the Academy of Performing Arts in Prague.

A beginning puppeteer should learn not only as much as possible about the craft of making the puppet, but also about the art of designing the puppet, the art of acting with the puppet, and the art of the theatre.

The goal of a puppeteer is the complete theatrical experience for his audience.

The performability of a good puppet is based on an inspired design, the perfect construction of even the simplest puppet, and the talent of the puppeteer.

A good puppet stage should appeal to the eyes of the audience without overwhelming the puppet. It should be simple, well-built, and fully serving the puppet play and the puppeteer.

When rehearsing, it's a good idea to have somebody who understands puppets sit outside and advise—if not on the concept (which is the director's role), at least on the understandability and cleanliness of the puppet movement.

Is there anything in the puppet world that really bugs you? The first problem in American puppetry seems to be lack of knowledge of theatre and design. What we usually see is a cute puppet show rather than *puppet theatre*. The scripts lack dramatic development in the story and in the characters. The second problem is too much sensitivity to one's creation. Puppeteers usually don't ask for, don't care for, and don't accept constructive criticism, all of which are important to the puppeteer's growth. If somebody tells you "It was nice," or worse, "It was cute," for the sake of puppetry ask him, "What do you mean?"

Appendix:

Puppet Guilds Affiliated with the Puppeteers of America, Inc.

ATLANTA SOUTHEASTERN PUPPETRY GUILD
Andy Bremer, President . . . . .287 Sherwood Rd., Smyrna, GA 30080
BOSTON AREA GUILD OF PUPPETRY
Stephen Babcock, President . . . . .45 Rutland St., Boston, MA 02118
CENTRAL COAST PUPPETRY GUILD
Judy F. Sims, President . . . . .5593 W. Camino Cielo, Santa Barbara, CA 93105
CENTRAL TEXAS PUPPET GUILD
Terry Tannert, President . . . . .2201 Forest Trail, Austin, TX 78703
CHICAGOLAND PUPPETRY GUILD
Ray Nelson, President . . . . .4220 S. Wallace Ave., Chicago, IL 60609
CINCINNATI AREA PUPPETRY GUILD
Kathy Piper, President . . . . .12013 State Rd. 521, Sunbury, OH 43074
COLUMBIA ASSOCIATION OF PUPPETEERS
Jeff Knight, President .Route #1, Box 265, Beavercreek, OR 97004
COLUMBUS PUPPETRY GUILD
Alice Rhodes, President . . . . .6820 Bowerman St., East Worthington, OH 43085
CONNECTICUT GUILD OF PUPPETRY
Michael Graham, President . . . . .200 Spring Valley Rd., Ridgefield, CT 06877
DETROIT PUPPETEERS GUILD
Brenda Hughes, President . . . . .1240 E. Long Lake Rd., Troy, MI 48098
FLORIDA SUNCOAST PUPPET GUILD
Virginia Rivers, President . . . . .6909 River Blvd., Tampa, FL 33604
GARDEN STATE PUPPETRY GUILD
Judith Caden, President . . . . .21 Glin Rd., West Orange, NJ 07052
GREATER HOUSTON PUPPETRY GUILD
Jean Kuecher, President . . . . .11610 Brookfalls Drive, Houston, TX 77070
HAWAII PUPPET GUILD
Anna M. Viggiano, President . . . . .94-186 Kupuna Loop, Waipahu, HI 96797
LONE STAR PUPPET GUILD
Fred Cowan, President . . . . .3018 Commerce St., Dallas, TX 75226
LOS ANGELES GUILD OF PUPPETRY
Frank Paris, President . . . . .7918 Babcock, North Hollywood, CA 91605
MILE HIGH PUPPETEERS
Ed Glassman, President . . . . .2416 Emerson St., Denver, CO 80205
NATIONAL CAPITAL PUPPETRY GUILD
Gail Cummins, President . . . . 47 S. Aberdeen St., Arlington, VA 22204
ORANGE COUNTY PUPPETRY GUILD
Janine Wright, President . . . . .520 W. Hill Ave., Fullerton, CA 92632
PHOENIX GUILD OF PUPPETRY
Bartlett Beebe, President . . . . .2330 E. Alameda Drive, Tempe, AZ 85282
PRAIRIE GUILD OF PUPPETRY
Veronika Ruedenberg, President . . . . .2834 Ross Rd., Ames, IA 50010
PUNCHINELLO PUPPETEERS GUILD
Janet Cooke, President . . . . .5190 Halifax Drive, San Jose, CA 95130

PUPPET GUILD OF GREATER MIAMI
    Charles Shaw Joss, President ....4200 Park Lane, West Palm Beach, FL 33406
PUPPET GUILD OF LONG ISLAND
    Rob Boehm, President ....21 Poplar Ave., South Farmingdale, NY 11735
PUPPET GUILD OF ST. LOUIS
    Ginny Weiss, President ....13016 Montmarte, St. Louis, MO 63141
PUPPETRY GUILD OF THE CAROLINAS
    Bob Pierce, President ....2700 Flintridge Drive, Charlotte, NC 28212
PUPPETRY GUILD OF GREATER NEW YORK, INC.
    Steven Widerman, President ......................P.O. Box 244, New York, NY 10116
PUPPETRY GUILD OF NORTHEASTERN OHIO
    Joe McCormack, President ....856 Rose Blvd., Highland Heights, OH 44143
QUAKER VILLAGE PUPPETEERS
    Sally Ream, President ....131 Pennell Rd., Glen Riddle, PA 19037
SAN DIEGO GUILD OF PUPPETRY
    Pam McIntyre, President ....2050 Chicago St., San Diego, CA 92110
SAN FRANCISCO BAY AREA PUPPETEERS GUILD
    Lettie Connell Schubert, President ....·.............14 Eton Way, Mill Valley, CA 94941
SAVANNAH COASTAL PUPPETRY GUILD
    Jewell G. Perkins, President ....1150 Shawnee St., Savannah, GA 31406
TWIN CITIES PUPPETEERS
    Kathy O'Brien, President ....2010 Bush St., St. Paul, MN 55119
VANCOUVER GUILD OF PUPPETRY
    Fran Dowie, President ..5491 Walton Rd., Richmond, British Columbia, Canada V7C 2L7

GUILDS WORKING ON CHARTER REQUIREMENTS—

OZARKS AREA PUPPETRY GUILD
    Nancy Spaeder, President ....1044 E. Normal St., Springfield, MO 65807
PUPPETRY GUILD OF UPSTATE NEW YORK
    Michael Oltz, President ....314 E. Seneca St., #101, Ithaca, NY 14850
SANTA CLARITA VALLEY GUILD OF PUPPETRY
    Mary Gallant, President ....27919 Bernina Ave., Canyon Country, CA 91351
SEATTLE PUPPET GUILD
    Jean Mattson, President ....13002-10th St. NW, Seattle, WA 98177

DIVISION OF REGIONS

NORTHEAST: Connecticut, Delaware, Maine, Maryland, Massachusetts, New Hampshire, New Jersey, New York, Pennsylvania, Rhode Island, Vermont, District of Columbia.

EASTERN CANADA: New Brunswick, Newfoundland, Nova Scotia, Ontario, Quebec.

SOUTHEAST: Alabama, Arkansas, Florida, Georgia, Kentucky, Louisiana, Mississippi, North Carolina, South Carolina, Tennessee, Virginia, West Virginia, Puerto Rico.

GREAT LAKES: Illinois, Indiana, Michigan, Ohio, Wisconsin.

GREAT PLAINS: Colorado, Iowa, Kansas, Manitoba, Minnesota, Missouri, Nebraska, North Dakota, South Dakota, Saskatchewan, Wyoming.

SOUTHWEST: New Mexico, Oklahoma, Republic of Mexico, Texas.

PACIFIC NORTHWEST: Alaska, Alberta, British Columbia, Idaho, Montana, Oregon, Washington.

PACIFIC SOUTHWEST: Arizona, California, Hawaii, Nevada, Utah.

British Puppetry Organizations

BRITISH PUPPET & MODEL THEATRE GUILD
Gordon Shapley, Hon. Sec. . . . . .18 Maple Rd., Yeading, Hayes, Middlesex, UB4 9LP
BRUNIMA (AN INTERNATIONAL ORGANIZATION)
Tom Howard, Hon. Sec. . . . . .5 Greystoke Gardens, Enfield, Middlesex
PUPPET CENTRE TRUST
Battersea Arts Centre . . . . .Lavender Hill, London, SW11 5TJ

Australian Puppetry Guilds

UNIMA (AUSTRALIAN CENTRE)
NEW SOUTH WALES SECTION
Norman Hetherington, President . . . . .17 Sirius Cove Rd., Mosmon 2088
WESTERN AUSTRALIA SECTION OF GUILD
Nancy Johnson, Secretary . . . . .54 Ord St., West Perth 6005
VICTORIA SECTION OF GUILD
A. Axelrad, President . . . . .Coonara Rd.,Olinda 3788
L. Gardener, Treasurer . . . . .72 Heathwood St., Ringwood East 3135